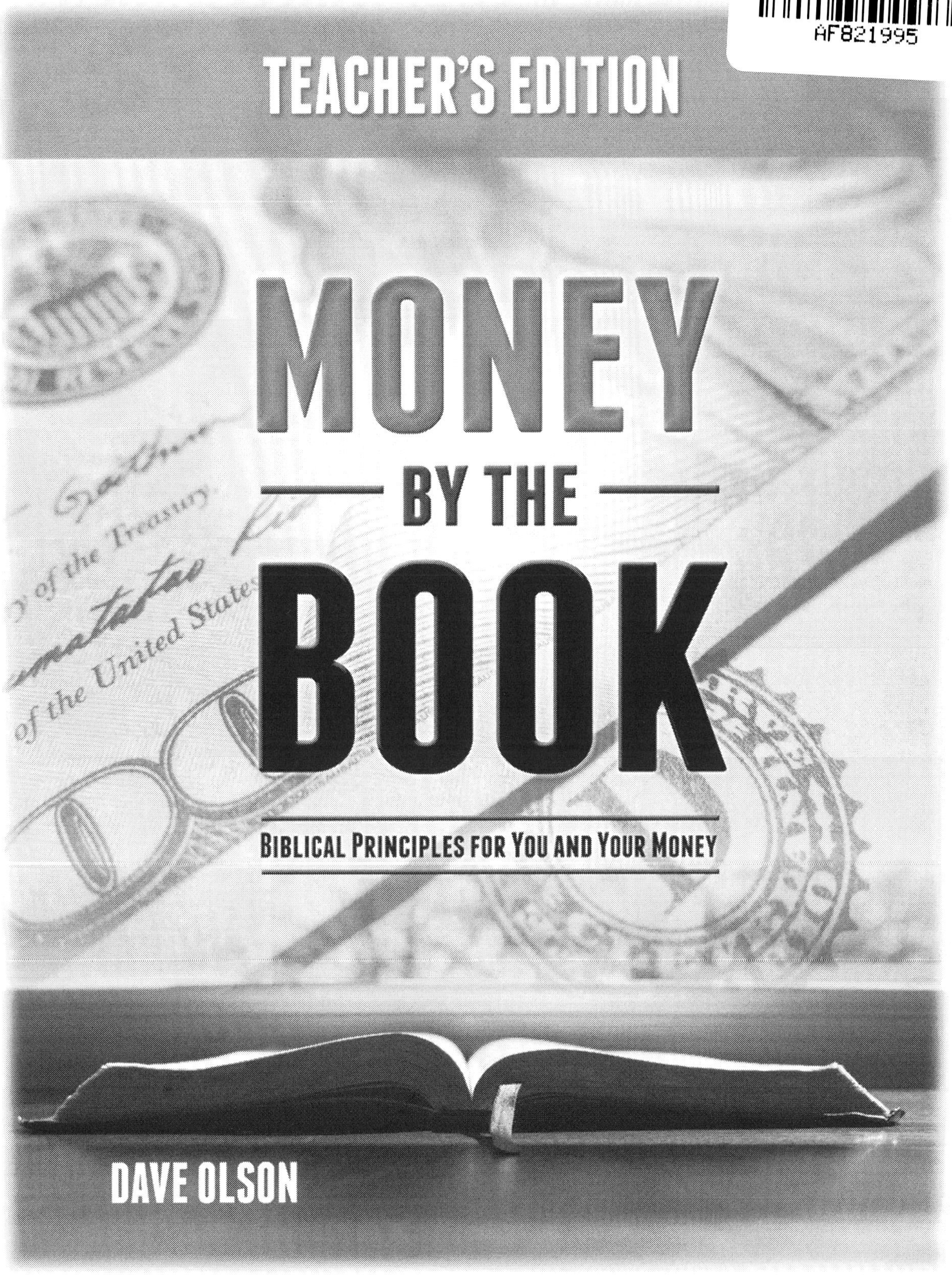

Published by
HELP4U PUBLICATIONS
CHESTERTON, IN

Help4U Publications, LLC
Chesterton, IN 46304

ISBN 978-1-940089-46-1

www.Help4Upublications.com

All Scripture quotations are from the *King James Bible*.

Contents

Instructions for Teachers

Thank you for choosing *Money by the Book: Teacher's Edition.* This book will enable you to teach others about the Biblical principles of money management. It has been adapted from *Money by the Book* and put in outline form, making it easy to teach in a group setting. Whether used as a college class, adult Sunday School curriculum, or as a series in a mid-week service, the truths discussed with your students will change their perspective about money and help them to achieve financial stability. Review questions at the end of each chapter are provided to challenge students to consider what has been taught.

Before starting your lectures, determine how many weeks you plan to teach. Then, consider the material found in each chapter. Although the book has eighteen chapters, it does not mean that you will teach one chapter per week for eighteen weeks. Lengthy chapters can be divided into two lessons, while shorter chapters can be combined into one lesson. A little planning at the beginning of the course should enable you to cover all of the material in a balanced manner.

A column is provided on each lecture page for you to record your own personal notes, examples, comments, or explanations. Since this is an adaptation of *Money by the Book*, many of the examples in the lessons are illustrations from my life. Therefore, consider substituting some of the stories with your own experiences. It will reinforce your authority on the subject matter, and your listeners will appreciate the personal anecdotes.

Students can benefit by taking notes and answering the review questions in the *Money by the Book: Student Guide.*

GOD HAS A PLAN FOR YOU AND YOUR MONEY

Key Verse: *"The rich ruleth over the poor, and the borrower is servant to the lender"* (Proverbs 22:7).

NOTES

1. MONEY DOES NOT BRING HAPPINESS

- Throughout history money has made some people extremely happy and others terribly miserable. Contrary to popular belief, an abundance of wealth does not always bring satisfaction. Often it leads to emptiness and despair. When a movie star commits suicide, it serves as a reminder that riches do not satisfy. It is not the amount of cash you possess that determines your happiness but your attitude toward it.

2. MONEY MUST BE MANAGED.

- Because money only goes so far, we all have to learn to use it wisely. God has established principles in the Bible to properly equip His people to manage their money. Believe it or not, God actually has a plan for your money. Since the earth is the Lord's, everything you own ultimately belongs to Him. You are merely a manager who needs divine wisdom to oversee what you have been given. Accordingly, each of us should strive to be a "faithful and wise steward" (Luke 12:42).

3. GOD TELLS US HOW TO MANAGE OUR MONEY.

- Those who properly handle their finances enjoy peace, stability, and sufficiency. However, failure to follow the Lord's guidelines always results in financial trouble. In fact, the difference between a peaceful marriage and a contentious one can hinge on how a couple manages their money. It is vital, therefore, to discover the truths that God has given to help us with our finances. Once you begin to follow His precepts, you will be amazed at how your economic situation will improve. As you carefully consider each chapter, you will discover several tips that will enable you to make the most of your money.

4. Learn practical principles.

- The goal of this book is twofold: to present Biblical principles regarding money and to provide practical suggestions for implementing those principles. It is difficult to present everything one needs to know about money in a single volume. Hopefully, you will be inspired to research matters of interest in a more thorough manner.

Note to Teacher: It is unfortunate that many people in our society look for others to blame for their problems. As a result, some people take legal action against organizations that seek to help them. Consider issuing a disclaimer at the beginning of your lesson to protect yourself from potential legal action. Here is an example:

> *The content of these lessons is for educational and informational purposes only. Opinions and suggestions are not intended to be nor should they be considered financial, tax, legal, or medical advice. The instructors and author of these lessons are not registered professional financial advisers, consultants, analysts, or planners, nor are they attorneys. They are not responsible for any financial or legal decisions made by the listeners. None of the content of these lessons should be deemed as financial or legal advice. Before following ideas presented in these lessons, diligent research and professional consultation should be made by each individual. You are fully responsible for your own financial decisions.*

NOTES

Chapter One

Be Content

Key Verse: *"Let your conversation be without covetousness; and be content with such things as ye have: for he hath said, I will never leave thee, nor forsake thee"* (Hebrews 13:5).

Introductory Thoughts:

- Contentment is one of the most important factors to consider in personal finances because a lack of contentment leads to covetousness and overspending.
- In reality, most money problems begin with a wrong attitude in the heart. Therefore, we must learn to guard against covetousness and cultivate contentment.
- As light and darkness cannot exist together, neither can covetousness and contentment.
- Benjamin Franklin said, "Money never made a man happy yet, nor will it. The more a man has, the more he wants. Instead of filling a vacuum, it makes one."[1]
- Before considering how we can develop contentment, let's understand what hinders a contented life.

1. The Enemies of Contentment

- Because God desires His people to be content, we can be certain that Satan seeks the opposite for our lives.
- The devil has two powerful weapons at his disposal to create a spirit of discontentment in the human heart: covetousness and entitlement.

a. Covetousness

- Very few people in life are satisfied with what they have. Covetousness has such a tight grip on their heart that they do not even see it as a problem.

Notes

- Illustration – Dave Olson recalled how he tried to explain covetousness to a young lady in her mid-twenties, and she said something like, "What's wrong with wanting what somebody else has? How's that a sin?" He couldn't believe what he had just heard! He had to explain to her that "Thou shalt not covet" (Exodus 20:17) is one of the Ten Commandments, and disobeying God is sin.
- Covetousness leads to misplaced priorities, overspending, and debt. The apostle Paul believed it was so terrible that he called it "idolatry" (Colossians 3:5). Anytime you place too much emphasis on something, it becomes an idol. Unfortunately, covetousness has become one of those "acceptable" sins committed by Christians; but we are commanded, ". . . let it not be once named among you" (Ephesians 5:3). Not once! Jesus said, "Take heed, and beware of covetousness: for a man's life consisteth not in the abundance of the things which he possesseth" (Luke 12:15). If Jesus warned us about it, shouldn't we beware? Life is not a contest to see who can accumulate the most stuff.
- Continually looking at things you don't have can create a longing for them. If you spend enough time going to a car dealership "just looking," before you know it, you will be driving a new car off the lot. Window shopping often turns into purchasing. Those who shop online are one click away from buying things they don't need and racking up more debt. It's no wonder that the Lord says, "beware."
- Although spending money is not wrong, it can easily become an addiction. We have all heard of people who jokingly say that they are shopaholics. What they really mean is that they are covetous, and that is no joking matter. It is a sin which leads to bondage.

b. Entitlement

- People who are covetous cannot always get the things they want. So, the ugly stepsister of Covetousness, named Entitlement, steps in and convinces people that they have a right to have what others have.

NOTES

- We are living in an age that many expect to be given what others have had to work hard to get.
- Citizens are told they deserve health insurance, free education, and income equality. People expect government handouts to pay for school lunches, housing, and groceries. A typical woman with five children out of wedlock believes that society should support her and her children. To her, it doesn't matter if everybody else has to work hard and sacrifice to provide for their children. She wants it and Entitlement has whispered in her ear that she deserves to have it.
- The typical kid has been infected with "entitlement-itis," too. How many children have smart phones and tablets? They think that because their parents have them, they deserve them as well. Because parents are so affected by covetousness, they fail to see its influence on their children. When those children grow up and get married, they think that they deserve to have the same lifestyle that their parents worked decades to achieve. What is the result? You guessed it—debt. Multitudes of young married couples go head over heels in debt because they want a big house, nice furniture, and a new car. Their lack of contentment creates problems that will take years from which to recover.

2. The Path to Contentment

- The opposite of covetousness is contentment. We are exhorted, "*Let your* conversation *be* without covetousness; *and be* content with such things as ye have: for he hath said, I will never leave thee, nor forsake thee" (Hebrews 13:5).
- Being content refers to being satisfied. Satisfaction goes beyond merely refraining from complaining about what God has provided; it realizes that God's provisions are always sufficient.

a. Be Thankful

- Contentment is directly tied to thankfulness. We stop being content when we cease being grateful for the many blessings God has bestowed upon us. It is difficult to be covetous and full of complaints when you are thankful. As is usually the case, failure to be full of the right thing is an invitation to the wrong thing to enter your life. A

Notes

thankful heart expresses appreciation for what it has without focusing on what it does not have.

- Isn't it amazing how you can be content with your living room furniture until your friend gets a new set of couches? Rather than let your eyes disturb your contentment, learn to thank God for His blessing upon others. Strike up a song of praise the next time you feel tempted to complain about your allotted portion. Cry as did the psalmist, "I will offer to thee the sacrifice of thanksgiving, and will call upon the name of the LORD" (Psalm 116:17).
- In Paul's life, he experienced times of plenty and seasons of scarceness. However, his joy never depended upon what he possessed. He said, "Not that I speak in respect of want: for I have learned, in whatsoever state I am, *therewith* to be content. I know both how to be abased, and I know how to abound: every where and in all things I am instructed both to be full and to be hungry, both to abound and to suffer need" (Philippians 4:11-12). He was happy with much and happy with a little. Can you say that describes your attitude toward things?
- Notice also that Paul said, "I have learned . . . to be content." What teaches us to be content? In addition to the Scriptures, experience is a wonderful instructor. Paul learned that God was faithful whether he was hungry or full. Learn to rejoice in the Lord during times of plenty and times of poverty. Contentment is something that must be learned; and if you never acquired it as a child, you will have to learn it as an adult. Whether the Lord fills your cupboards or allows them to be bare, realize that He is teaching you an important lesson in contentment. "Rejoice in the Lord alway: *and* again I say, Rejoice" (Philippians 4:4).

b. Focus on Necessities

- Every Christian must learn to be satisfied with two basic necessities: food and clothing.
- "And having food and raiment let us be therewith content" (1 Timothy 6:8).
- Anything more is actually a luxury. In America, most would argue with this point; but many people in

NOTES

developing nations are satisfied if they have food in their stomach and an extra set of clothes.

- Unfortunately, living in the land of plenty has made us forget that we are not entitled to being rich.
- This entitlement generation demands everything from everybody.
- When parents give children everything they want and government gives its citizens never-ending handouts, they destroy the spirit of contentment.
- We must all learn to be satisfied with the basic necessities of life.

NOTES

c. Avoid Jealousy

- There will always be people who have more than you have, so refuse to become envious of others.
- You may feel the pressure to keep up with your peers, but that is vain.
- The Lord reminds us, "A little that a righteous man hath *is* better than the riches of many wicked" (Psalm 37:16).
- Your *little* is better than their *riches.* In fact, in most cases, the person you envy is in debt and suffering from the associated strife and bondage that indebtedness brings.
- Solomon reminds us, "Better *is* an handful *with* quietness, than both the hands full *with* travail and vexation of spirit" (Ecclesiastes 4:6).
- Both of the two verses we have just considered have a common key word—*better.* Learn that God's way of contentedness is far better than the world's infatuation with covetousness.
- Having both hands full prevents you from enjoying what you have. You always need one hand free.

d. Guard Your Attitude

- Having money is not a problem, but having a wrong attitude concerning it will create much trouble. Paul warned Timothy, "For the love of money is the root of all evil: which while some coveted after, they have erred from the faith, and pierced themselves through with many sorrows" (1 Timothy 6:10). Money is not evil, but having an insatiable craving for it will lead to sin. People lie, steal, and kill for money. Marriages are weakened and children are neglected by couples seeking more income. It is easy to see that a love for money ruins individuals, families, and society. Further, those who have an unquenchable appetite for wealth are *pierced . . . with many sorrows.* Much unnecessary heartache can be prevented by maintaining a right attitude toward money.

- Let's consider the proper mind-set to have about money. King Solomon said, "Labour not to be rich: cease from thine own wisdom. Wilt thou set thine eyes upon that which is not? for *riches* certainly make themselves wings; they fly away as an eagle toward heaven" (Proverbs 23:4-5). This passage teaches three things.

1) The goal of working is not to become rich.
    - *"Labour not to be rich."* Society is filled with get-rich-quick schemes. People want to make the most amount of money doing the least amount of work.
    - Scripture teaches that we should work hard to provide for our families, give to the Lord, and be a blessing to others in need.
    - Having a goal of getting rich is not Biblical. However, that does not mean that being wealthy is sinful.
    - The Lord certainly likes to bless His people, and many godly people have been showered with much of this world's goods.
    - It is not wealth but the desire for riches that is sinful.
2) Wealth is often elusive.
    - Solomon warned us not to set our *eyes upon that which is not.*
    - Most who desire to be rich never actually become wealthy. They waste their time looking for something that will never come to pass. Then, because they fail to seek the Lord, they miss the true treasures that God wants to give to them.
    - Why long for *that which is not* when you can set your eyes upon God?
3) Money does not last long.
    - Money tends to leave as quickly as it comes.
    - Sometimes people spend money before they even have it. Riches truly grow wings and *fly away.*

NOTES

- It seems unwise to spend so much time trying to gather something that lasts for such a short amount of time. It is better to seek things that will last for eternity.

Concluding Thoughts:

✓ Many books have been written on the topic of personal finances.

✓ Unfortunately, after reading some of those books, readers become excited about getting their finances under control for the purpose of becoming rich.

✓ After seeing the possibilities of wealth building, they say to themselves, "If I follow this plan, I will be a millionaire when I retire; and then I can do the things I've always dreamed about doing."

✓ While we have an obligation to be good stewards, we must be careful that we do not set goals based upon covetousness.

✓ Although investing is important, our focus should be to prepare for future needs, not necessarily to become filthy rich.

Review Questions

1. What are the two enemies of contentment? covetousness, entitlement
2. How are people affected by having an attitude of entitlement? They think that they deserve handouts without having to work.
3. How can being thankful prevent covetousness? It is difficult to complain when praising God.
4. What are the two basic necessities mentioned in 1 Timothy 6:8? food, raiment (clothing)
5. Does the Bible encourage us to work in order to get rich? No Support your answer with Scripture. Proverbs 23:4-5

---

[1] Rob Berger, "Top 100 Money Quotes of All Time," *Forbes*, accessed May 20, 2015, http://www.forbes.com/sites/robertberger/2014/04/30/top-100-money-quotes-of-all-time/.

Notes

Chapter Two

Don't Fall for the Prosperity Gospel

Notes

Key Verse: *"I marvel that ye are so soon removed from him that called you into the grace of Christ unto another gospel: Which is not another; but there be some that trouble you, and would pervert the gospel of Christ"* (Galatians 1:6-7).

Introductory Thoughts:

- Somehow, people think that living for God will make all of their problems go away. All they need to do is read the Bible for a while, and they will soon discover that those who follow the Lord often face opposition, deprivation, and suffering.
- David was hunted by thousands. Moses was hated by the very people he was called to lead. James and John were asked to give up their financial security and forsake their fishing business. The apostle Paul not only lost his health—he also lost his head.
- Multitudes have fallen prey to the teachings associated with the prosperity gospel. The reasoning of many goes like this: "God is love; and because He loves me, He would not want me to suffer physically or financially. Therefore, it is His will for me to be healthy and rich."
- While promises of health and wealth are appealing, they are not Biblical.
- The promoters of the prosperity gospel have been around for a long time, stressing that riches are a sign of holiness. Even in Paul's day people had to deal with such false teaching. That is why Paul warned of "men of corrupt minds" who taught that "gain is godliness" (1 Timothy 6:5).
- Let's consider a few reasons why we should reject the prosperity gospel.

1. It is a False Gospel

- The word *gospel* means good news.

- According to Mark, we are commanded to "preach the gospel to every creature" (Mark 16:15). But just which gospel are we to preach? The apostle Paul clearly defined the gospel as the death, burial, and resurrection of Jesus. "Moreover, brethren, I declare unto you the gospel which I preached unto you, which also ye have received, and wherein ye stand . . . how that Christ died for our sins according to the scriptures; And that he was buried, and that he rose again the third day according to the scriptures" (1 Corinthians 15:1-4). The gospel, therefore, is the good news of salvation through Jesus.
- Nowhere in Scripture is the word *gospel* ever used in connection with gaining money, riches, wealth, or material blessings. It is NEVER used in such a way.
- The Galatian people faced a false gospel of another sort. They were wrongly taught by ignorant men that salvation required following the Old Testament Law.
- Paul emphatically warned them not to receive any gospel but the true one: "I marvel that ye are so soon removed from him that called you into the grace of Christ unto another gospel: Which is not another; but there be some that trouble you, and would pervert the gospel of Christ. But though we, or an angel from heaven, preach any other gospel unto you than that which we have preached unto you, let him be accursed" (Galatians 1:6-8).
- From this passage we see that *another gospel* is to be rejected because those who preach it *pervert the gospel of Christ* and *trouble you.* Such a serious offense demands strong condemnation, and Paul gave that, too. Anyone who preached a gospel that he had not preached was to *be accursed.*
- It is a terrible manipulation of Scripture to substitute the promise of riches for the promise of salvation.

2. It is Promoted by False Prophets

- It makes sense that a false gospel is preached by false prophets.
- Promoters of the prosperity gospel do not focus on preaching repentance and the need of forgiveness of sin through the shed blood of Christ. Instead, they promise material blessings through "faith in Jesus." The problem is that their

Notes

false gospel also paints a different picture of Jesus than we see in the Bible.

- Paul warned that people would preach "another Jesus, whom we have not preached" and "another gospel" (2 Corinthians 11:4). Their "Jesus" is tolerant of sin and willing to bless anybody who is willing to ask for assistance. Because he is gracious, he makes no demands of holy living and does not confront people with their sin.
- Preachers who fail to call sinners to repentance are not sent by God. Listen to the Lord's own testimony: "I have not sent these prophets . . . . But if they had stood in my counsel, and had caused my people to hear my words, then they should have turned them from their evil way, and from the evil of their doings" (Jeremiah 23:21-22).
- So, if preachers fail to challenge people to turn from their sinful ways, they are not speaking for the Lord. Therefore, they are speaking lies, and that makes them false prophets.
- It appears that the prosperity gospel works for some—the false prophets! Titus was warned that there were "many unruly and vain talkers and deceivers" who were "teaching things which they ought not, for filthy lucre's sake" (Titus 1:10-11). The fact remains that men preach a false gospel in order to make money. While describing false prophets, Peter said, "And through covetousness shall they with feigned words make merchandise of you" (2 Peter 2:3). In many cases, the only ones who actually get rich are the preachers who twist the Scriptures for their own benefits.
- You do not have to listen to false teachers to develop a tendency to think that you deserve blessings. We all have something in common with every false prophet—sinful flesh. Our sin nature is naturally selfish and craves to be satisfied. Nobody is immune to the prosperity gospel.

3. It Encourages Covetousness

- Jesus warned, "Take heed, and beware of covetousness" (Luke 12:15).
- It is not God's will for any of His children to have an insatiable appetite to gain more of this world's goods. Our affection should be "on things above, not on things on the earth" (Colossians 3:2). However, the prosperity gospel compels followers to focus on material blessings.

Notes

- The attitude promoted by the prosperity preachers is covetousness, but they call it "the gospel." This is the epitome of calling evil good.
- Christ taught, "It is more blessed to give than to receive" (Acts 20:35). What is the focus of the prosperity gospel: giving or receiving? Obviously, it is receiving. So, once again, the entire premise of this popular movement is proven to be against the teaching of Christ.
- A true believer enjoys giving to God and to others in need; but covetous people always have an expectant eye, hoping to receive something in return. While it is true that God does give to those who are generous, He does not promise to bless covetous people. Why would He bless sin?
- Consider the parable of the sower and the seeds that fell among the thorns. "And that which fell among thorns are they, which, when they have heard, go forth, and are choked with cares and riches and pleasures of *this* life, and bring no fruit to perfection" (Luke 8:14). What happened to the seeds? They were choked by the thorns. What were the thorns? They were the *cares and riches and pleasures of this life.* Instead of promoting Christian growth, the prosperity gospel seeks to entangle people with thorns that will choke the Word of God. The result is fruitlessness. Does that sound like a good gospel? Certainly not!
- Covetousness is sin, and calling it "the gospel" does not make it right. Wrapping covetousness in a cloak of spirituality is a doctrine promoted by devils.
- God promises to supply our needs, not all of our wants. If the Lord wants us to be content with food and clothing (1 Timothy 6:8), the prosperity preachers should not teach that we have a right to have more. Without Scriptural basis, they say that it is God's will for every faithful believer to be wealthy.
- Save yourself a lot of grief and disappointment by refusing to be duped into accepting this false gospel.

4. It Belittles the Poor

- According to the prosperity crowd, material blessing is a sign of being close to God. If that is true, some of the men we consider to be great in the Bible were actually out of fellowship with the Lord.

NOTES

- John the Baptist was not rich but lived in the wilderness eating bugs and wearing rough clothing. Elisha was a common farmer when he was called to be a prophet. Despite being "perfect and upright, and one that feared God," Job lost all of his earthly possessions (Job 1:1). Paul had to make tents on his missionary journeys to help support himself. Peter was so poor that Jesus had to perform a miracle to help him pay his taxes. Although Onesimus was a poor slave, his Christian character was highly regarded. What about Jesus? He said, "The foxes have holes, and the birds of the air *have* nests; but the Son of man hath not where to lay *his* head" (Matthew 8:20). Because our Lord greatly lacked this world's goods, He did not even have a place to lay His head at night. Are we to believe that all of these great men of God and Jesus Himself were deprived of material blessings due to flawed character or insufficient faith? Nonsense!
- The prosperity gospel ignores God's clear teachings about poor people. The word *poor* is found almost two hundred times in the Bible. Observe the Lord's statement about His people: "For the poor shall never cease out of the land: therefore I command thee, saying, Thou shalt open thine hand wide unto thy brother, to thy poor, and to thy needy, in thy land" (Deuteronomy 15:11). Rather than say that all people could become rich, He clearly said that there would always be poor people in the land. Further, He did not promise to make them all rich. Instead, He commanded His people to take care of their brethren.
- It seems almost universally accepted that poverty is a bad thing. These days, our government officials talk about "income inequality" and the injustices of some having more than others. However, we should not believe the lie that those who are not rich are poor. If you live in America, you are rich.
- <u>Illustration</u> – Having lived in a developing country for nearly a decade, Dave Olson saw true poverty. Interestingly enough, he also observed that many people with little of this world's goods are actually happier than those with an abundance.
- Have you ever wondered why Jesus told us to pray for our *daily bread*? He wants us to trust Him every day for our needs. Living "hand to mouth" is not a curse like many lead us to believe.

NOTES

- Jesus taught that we should trust Him for each day's provision. Those who are too comfortable financially miss out on leaning upon the Lord for their daily needs. With our fridges, freezers, and cupboards full, why would we need to ask God for today's meals? Having less often leads us to develop a closer relationship with the Lord as we seek Him to provide for us. In fact, the poor have a special opportunity to be rich in faith. "Hearken, my beloved brethren, Hath not God chosen the poor of this world rich in faith, and heirs of the kingdom which he hath promised to them that love him?" (James 2:5).
- Being poor is not necessarily a curse but may be a source of blessing to those who learn to trust God in their plight. Becoming rich with this world's goods is often more of a curse than a blessing because it can drive people further from God instead of closer to Him.
- I am certainly not advocating that everybody should give all of their money away and become poor in order to be blessed. However, I do believe that God uses poverty to draw many closer to Himself, and those who trust Him will become *rich in faith.*

5. It Detracts from the True Riches

- Someone has aptly said, "The best things in life are not things." Unfortunately, the prosperity preachers emphasize that gain is godliness. They suppose that the riches we should seek in this life are money and material possessions. However, that is a shallow view of heavenly blessing.
- On the contrary, Christ spoke of a nobler sort of riches. "If therefore ye have not been faithful in the unrighteous mammon, who will commit to your trust the true *riches*?" (Luke 16:11). Mammon refers to money, but Jesus mentioned something far better—*the true riches.* This indicates that not all references to riches and blessings in the Bible refer to money.
- When we read the Bible incorrectly and focus on money every time we see the word *riches*, we can get a distorted view of the subject.
- Solomon understood that a man could be poor and rich at the same time. He said, "There is that maketh himself rich, yet *hath* nothing: *there is* that maketh himself poor, yet *hath* great riches" (Proverbs 13:7). A rich man may have a lot of

Notes

cash but be missing the most important riches of all, and a man with little can possess tremendous wealth. For instance, a man might sacrifice to provide a Christian education for his children. Instead of owning a large home and a new car, he invests in something far greater—his children. Who is better off: the one with a large bank account or the one who watches his children grow up to serve the Lord? Obviously, the latter.

- Notice once again the wording of Scripture: "A faithful man shall abound with blessings" (Proverbs 28:20). Does it say that a faithful man will abound with money or riches? No, it says, *blessings.* Do not allow people to twist the Scripture to serve their purposes.
- As you study the Scripture, you will begin to realize what the true riches of this life are. Consider the following:

a. **Salvation through Christ –** "To whom God would make known what *is* the riches of the glory of this mystery among the Gentiles; which is Christ in you, the hope of glory" (Colossians 1:27).

b. **Faith –** "Hearken, my beloved brethren, Hath not God chosen the poor of this world rich in faith, and heirs of the kingdom which he hath promised to them that love him?" (James 2:5).

c. **Forgiveness and Grace –** "In whom we have redemption through his blood, the forgiveness of sins, according to the riches of his grace" (Ephesians 1:7).

d. **Spiritual Strength –** "That he would grant you, according to the riches of his glory, to be strengthened with might by his Spirit in the inner man" (Ephesians 3:16).

e. **Children –** "Lo, children *are* an heritage of the LORD: *and* the fruit of the womb *is his* reward" (Psalm 127:3).

f. **A Godly Wife –** "House and riches *are* the inheritance of fathers: and a prudent wife *is* from the LORD" (Proverbs 19:14).

g. **The Goodness and Patience of God –** "Or despisest thou the riches of his goodness and forbearance and longsuffering; not knowing that the goodness of God leadeth thee to repentance?" (Romans 2:4).

h. **The Word of God –** "The law of thy mouth *is* better unto me than thousands of gold and silver" (Psalm 119:72).

i. **Wisdom and Knowledge –** "O the depth of the riches both of the wisdom and knowledge of God! how unsearchable *are*

NOTES

his judgments, and his ways past finding out!" (Romans 11:33).

j. **Assurance of Salvation –** "That their hearts might be comforted, being knit together in love, and unto all riches of the full assurance of understanding, to the acknowledgement of the mystery of God, and of the Father, and of Christ" (Colossians 2:2).

k. **Reproach and Suffering –** "Esteeming the reproach of Christ greater riches than the treasures in Egypt: for he had respect unto the recompence of the reward" (Hebrews 11:26).

- ➢ Don't forget to focus on the true riches.
- ➢ When your attention is upon the things of this world, you will pursue material blessings instead of spiritual ones.
- ➢ Satan does not only tempt weak people with worldly pleasures, he also seeks to distract even the most faithful followers of the Lord.
- ➢ Though any strong believer would denounce the prosperity gospel, he must also beware of its subtle influences. Many good people end up feeling sorry for themselves when hardships enter their lives.
- ➢ We cannot expect a "bed of roses" when our Savior experienced a crown of thorns.

CONCLUDING THOUGHTS:

- ✓ As we conclude our consideration of the prosperity gospel, I hope you are more convinced than ever to trust the Lord to meet your daily needs.
- ✓ Adhering to the notion that God will make you prosperous simply because you love Him is faulty.
- ✓ Do not think that being a child of God means that you will never face lean times or financial trials.
- ✓ The Lord often uses such situations to draw us closer to Himself.
- ✓ Instead of thinking God has failed you, run to Him for deliverance.

NOTES

Review Questions

1. Why is the prosperity gospel considered a false gospel? <u>In Scripture, the gospel message is not associated with gaining money, riches, or wealth.</u>
2. How does the prosperity gospel promote covetousness? <u>It creates an insatiable appetite for more of this world's goods.</u>
3. How does the prosperity gospel belittle the poor? <u>It implies that they are not godly enough to be blessed with wealth.</u>
4. List some of the true riches mentioned in Scripture. <u>salvation, faith, forgiveness, strength, family, the goodness of God, Word of God, suffering</u>
5. How can you pursue the true riches? <u>answers will vary – seek things above, not things on earth</u>

Chapter Three

Give to God (Part 1: His Method)

Key Verse: *"Bring ye all the tithes into the storehouse, that there may be meat in mine house, and prove me now herewith, saith the* LORD *of hosts, if I will not open you the windows of heaven, and pour you out a blessing, that there shall not be room enough to receive it"* (Malachi 3:10).

Introductory Thoughts:

- Many people misunderstand the importance of giving. Worldly skeptics like to say that tithing is something that preachers and churches created to scam people out of their hard-earned money. Some are so stingy that their motto is "A dollar given is a dollar lost." However, no Christian has ever lost by giving back to God a portion of what he has been given.
- It is important for every believer to understand that their financial condition is directly related to their giving. As we will see, those who give are blessed, and those who don't give are cursed. Unfortunately, many of God's people struggle with giving to the Lord. Even those who know they should give find excuse after excuse for not being faithful.
- Whether you are consistent with your giving or struggle with it, this chapter has something in it for you. So, let's learn some valuable truths as we consider a few questions about giving.

1. Who Is Supposed to Give?

- Giving is not merely an Old Testament doctrine as some suggest. It is very prevalent in the New Testament also. Believers in every dispensation have given to God out of a heart of gratitude. Let's consider a couple categories of people that God expects to give.

a. The Rich Should Give

- This may seem obvious to most of us, but many rich people give sparingly.

Notes

- Consider the instructions given to Timothy by Paul: "Charge them that are rich in this world, that they be not highminded, nor trust in uncertain riches, but in the living God, who giveth us richly all things to enjoy; That they do good, that they be rich in good works, ready to distribute, willing to communicate" (1 Timothy 6:17-18).
- The wealthy believers in the church of Ephesus were not only expected to give but commanded to do so. All who are *rich in this world* should also be *rich in good works.* It is clear that those who have been entrusted with many of this world's goods should be *ready* and *willing* to part with some of them.
- It is not a sin to be rich. At times, the Lord pours material blessings upon His children. Abraham, David, and Solomon were all quite wealthy; but they were also liberal givers. For example, on one occasion Solomon offered a thousand burnt offerings. In his day, wealth was measured by the amount of cattle they owned, and parting with a thousand beasts was a significant offering. The point is that God may give you much so that you can give much.
- If you have been blessed financially, remember that God wants to channel money through you to support His work.

b. The Poor Should Give

- The progressives in our government believe that the rich should "foot the bill" for the poor. They expect the poor to give little to nothing by way of taxes. It is a socialistic philosophy. Unfortunately, people are bringing that mind-set into churches.
- In God's economy, everybody is expected to give to His work, not only the rich. The problem with so many Christians is that they look at giving as a tax that they owe God. How wrong they are!
- Giving is not a tax; it is an investment that always brings a return.
- Jesus taught, "Give, and it shall be given unto you" (Luke 6:38).
- To exclude the poor from giving would be to rob them of needed blessings. As we will see later, opportunities to give should be seen as a privilege, not a dreaded

NOTES

requirement. If God excused the poor from giving, they would be impoverished materially, emotionally, and spiritually.

- Consider the example of the poor believers in Macedonia. "Moreover, brethren, we do you to wit of the grace of God bestowed on the churches of Macedonia; How that in a great trial of affliction the abundance of their joy and their deep poverty abounded unto the riches of their liberality" (2 Corinthians 8:1-2). Observe who was responsible for their giving—it was God. He gave them the grace to be able to give when it seemed impossible to do so, and the same grace is available to all who need it today. How wonderful that the Lord enables us to do His will! Notice also that the people were in a *great trial of affliction.* This *great trial* refers to a time of testing. Rather than focusing on their own problems, these Christians decided to be a blessing through giving.
- Although the Macedonian believers suffered from *deep poverty,* they still gave. Few of us in America understand deep poverty.
- Illustration – While living in Zambia, Africa, as a missionary, Dave Olson witnessed people who were truly destitute. During his first year on the mission field, he saw true hunger. Due to a drought which occurred during the previous growing season, many had little to eat. Families went to the bush to dig for wild roots just to find something to eat. On one occasion, a woman with a baby strapped on her back went to his property in the midst of a steady rain, asking to work in his yard to earn enough money to buy food for her family for that day. Obviously, he did not make her work but gave her some food and a little money to take care of her pressing need. It was heartbreaking to see such desperation. In the midst of this difficult time, many of the poor people in his church still cheerfully gave to the Lord. One particular poor, elderly lady even gave a basket of sweet potatoes to the missionary family to express her love for them. These people did not use their poverty to be excused from giving. Compared to the poor saints in the church in Africa, you are quite rich.
- Whether you consider yourself rich or poor, you have an obligation to give.

NOTES

2. What Are We to Give?

- Now that we have seen that each of us should participate in giving, we will focus on what we should give.

a. Give Yourself

- When God has a man's heart, He also has his wallet.
- Those who refuse to yield to God will struggle in many areas of life, including giving.
- Let's consider again the poor Macedonian believers who gave so liberally. As you read the following passage, try to find the key that enabled them to give as they did. "For to *their* power, I bear record, yea, and beyond *their* power *they were* willing of themselves; Praying us with much intreaty that we would receive the gift, and *take upon us* the fellowship of the ministering to the saints. And *this they did*, not as we hoped, but first gave their own selves to the Lord, and unto us by the will of God" (2 Corinthians 8:3-5). Did you find the reason for their ability to give so sacrificially? Notice that they *first gave their own selves to the Lord.*
- When we give ourselves unreservedly to the Lord, He gets everything we own. For example, Abraham was willing to offer his son because he had first given himself to God.
- The problem with so many Christians is that they have given themselves to entertainment, covetousness, gossip, and the lusts of the flesh instead of yielding themselves to God. It is no wonder their giving is meager or with a wrong attitude.
- If preaching on giving causes you to bristle up and think that the preacher is just after more of your money, it is a good possibility that you have given your heart to something other than the Lord.
- Are you withholding some area of your life from God? If so, it will most certainly affect your financial situation. Give yourself unreservedly to God.
- "I beseech you therefore, brethren, by the mercies of God, that ye present your bodies a living sacrifice, holy, acceptable unto God, *which is* your reasonable service" (Romans 12:1).

Notes

NOTES

- After surrendering your will to God, giving will become easy.
- It is possible to give to the Lord without first giving Him your heart. We have a perfect example of this in the Scriptures. Ananias and Sapphira sold land and gave a portion of the proceeds to God. However, they lied and led people to believe that they had given the entire amount. Although they were not required to sell their property, they did; but it was for the wrong reason—they wanted the praise of man.
- Even today, people give so they can be approved of men. Like Ananias and Sapphira, some seek to look good in the eyes of the preacher. They give in hope of receiving prominence or position in the church. How wicked and deceitful!
- God primarily wants your heart, not your money. When He has your heart, you will give the right amount of money for the right reasons.

b. Give the Tithe

- Ten percent of all your income belongs to God. "And all the tithe of the land . . . *is* the LORD'S: *it is* holy unto the LORD" (Leviticus 27:30). The word *tithe* means 10 percent. Because the tithe belongs to God, it is not yours. In the prophet Malachi's day, many of God's people did not give their tithes; and the Lord confronted them, saying, "Will a man rob God? Yet ye have robbed me. But ye say, Wherein have we robbed thee? In tithes and offerings" (Malachi 3:8). Because God has given us everything that we own, we should gladly give Him the required 10 percent, along with an additional offering from a thankful heart. If you spend His tithe on something else, you are a thief. Notice God's words—*ye have robbed me.*
- Do not think that the Lord will bless your finances if you steal from Him.
- There are some Christians who believe that they are not obligated to give God a tithe, saying that it is an Old Testament doctrine. How convenient!
- Should we toss out other doctrines because they are found in the Old Testament? Are the Ten Commandments null and void simply because they are

recorded in the Old Testament? All of the practical wisdom contained in Proverbs and the comfort provided by the Psalms would also have to be disregarded because they are not New Testament books. The argument is completely unfounded.

- We would do well to remember Paul's exhortation, "All scripture *is* given by inspiration of God, and *is* profitable for doctrine, for reproof, for correction, for instruction in righteousness: That the man of God may be perfect, throughly furnished unto all good works" (2 Timothy 3:16-17). *All scripture* includes the Old Testament.
- It is true that not all things recorded in the Old Testament apply to us today. Some parts of the Law were exclusively for the children of Israel. For example, the Sabbath was instituted as a covenant between God and Israel. Other portions of the Law have been lifted. For instance, we are not required to offer animal sacrifices for our sin because Jesus came as the perfect Lamb of God, making a sacrifice that was "once *for all*" (Hebrews 10:10). Additionally, the dietary restrictions placed on the Jews have been lifted as seen in 1 Timothy 4:4-5, "For every creature of God *is* good, and nothing to be refused, if it be received with thanksgiving: For it is sanctified by the word of God and prayer." While we clearly have a New Testament passage of Scripture that lifts the dietary laws, we have no such passage that removes the responsibility to tithe. It simply does not exist. Nowhere did God say that tithing was only for the Israelites.
- To say that tithing is an Old Testament teaching does not mean it is not a New Testament teaching. While condemning the Pharisees for their hypocrisy, Jesus commended them for one thing—they tithed properly. Our Lord said, "Woe unto you, scribes and Pharisees, hypocrites! for ye pay tithe of mint and anise and cummin, and have omitted the weightier *matters* of the law, judgment, mercy, and faith: these ought ye to have done, and not to leave the other undone" (Matthew 23:23). They were condemned for refusing to exercise judgment, mercy, and faith. However, when it came to their many tithes, He said, "these ought ye to have done." It is clear that we *ought* to tithe.

NOTES

- Christ's words are enough proof for most of us that tithing is a practice found in the New Testament. However, some people argue that at the time Jesus spoke those words, the people were still following the Law. Therefore, according to them, it does not prove that tithing is supposed to be followed by Christians today. For those skeptics, we have further proof that tithing was practiced by New Testament believers after the death of Christ. The writer of Hebrews said, "And here men that die receive tithes" (Hebrews 7:8). Notice that the verb *receive* is in the present tense—meaning that at the time the book of Hebrews was written, people gave tithes.
- Some truths of Scripture transcend every dispensation. Murder was wrong before the Law; it was wrong during the Law; and it is still wrong after the Law. Marriage was instituted before the Law, practiced during the Law, and is a God-ordained institution after the Law. Likewise, tithing was practiced before the Law, during the Law, and after the Law.
- Some people suppose that living under the dispensation of grace relieves them from the duty of tithing. If anything, living under grace allows us to exceed the demands of the Law. As we have already seen, the Macedonian believers provide a wonderful example of this truth. How did they give in extreme poverty? They did it by grace! It was *the grace of God bestowed on the churches of Macedonia* that allowed them to give more abundantly than just a tithe.
- Unfortunately, most who argue that we are no longer required to give a tithe do not follow the example of the Macedonian believers. Instead, they want to justify their actions of robbing God.

c. Give an Offering

- Tithes and offerings are not the same.
- As we have already seen, the tithe is the Lord's. When you give a tithe, you have only given back to Him what is rightfully His.
- An offering is over and above the tithe. God deserves both.

NOTES

- Notice His expectations in Malachi 3:8, "Will a man rob God? Yet ye have robbed me. But ye say, Wherein have we robbed thee? In tithes and offerings."
- The example of a little girl who received ten shiny new pennies should challenge us all.[2] She picked up the first one and said, "This one is for Jesus." She continued saying, "And this one is for Mommy, and this one is for Daddy." She had a plan for all of her precious little coins. To her, it was a treasure. When she got to the last penny, she said, "And this one is for Jesus."
  Her mother replied, "But you already gave Him one."
  "Yes," she responded, "but that one belonged to Jesus. This one is a present."
- That little girl understood what many adults have never fully grasped. God deserves more than a tithe. He ought to get a present, too.
- Although the market is flooded with Christian books about finances, there is one glaring problem with many of them. When making a budget, they usually suggest only giving 10 percent of one's income to God. This is a grave mistake. If we set our budgets without including an offering, we will fail to give properly. God certainly deserves more than the tithe. How much more? The Bible does not say, and I believe that is purposeful. When the needs of your church are great, God may lead you to sacrifice and give more than you usually give. Sometimes, we are blessed with extra and are able to give of our abundance.
- Our attitude should not be, How much do I have to give? but How much am I able to give? If you are heavily in debt, you will be hindered from giving a large offering, but you must still give the tithe because it belongs to God.
- It is exciting to give an offering to God because of all that He has done for us.
- <u>Illustration</u> – Before Dave Olson got right with the Lord, he testifies that he gave more than 10 percent of his income to worldly pleasures; and now he would rather give more to God than he ever gave to sinful pursuits.
- In the Old Testament, people gave freewill offerings. They were "just because I want to" offerings.

NOTES

- When is the last time you gave something to God simply because your heart welled up with gratitude for Who He is and what He has done for you? Hopefully, you are not the type that calculates exactly what you "owe" God, believing that He should feel lucky when you give Him any extra.
- Consider one more illustration. After dining at a restaurant, the customary practice is to leave a tip for a waitress. Most people agree that the suggested amount of the tip should be between 15 and 20 percent of the total bill. Isn't it odd that many Christians treat their waitress better than they do God? Surely the Lord has done more for us than a waitress! Doesn't He deserve more than 10 percent?

NOTES

3. How Are We to Give?

- The Lord not only tells what to give, He also provides instructions for doing it. Let's consider the manner in which we should give.

a. Bountifully

- The stingy at heart are now saying, "Oh, there you go again—telling us to give a lot of money!" If that is your attitude, you have completely misunderstood God's intentions. After all, He owns the cattle on a thousand hills and does not need any of your meager gifts.
- A forgotten reason that God exhorts us to give is so that He can bless us for our faith and obedience.
- Consider the wonderful promise found in 2 Corinthians 9:6, "But this *I say*, He which soweth sparingly shall reap also sparingly; and he which soweth bountifully shall reap also bountifully." Notice that our reaping is in proportion to our sowing. Those who give sparingly receive little, but those who give much receive much in return. We actually determine how much God blesses us based on how we give. Such promises are not meant to create a desire for a big return from God but rather to be an assurance that He will meet our needs when we give sacrificially.
- Illustration – Years ago, Dave Olson worked in an engineering office. During that time, he earned the confidence of his employer and was given greater

responsibilities. The company had brought in private contractors who were paid quite well for their services, and it dawned on him that he was doing some of the same work as those contractors for a fraction of the pay. He began to feel sorry for himself and really wanted a raise. Realizing that his attitude was not right, he promised God that if he got a raise, he would give Him the entire portion of it as an added offering. Sure enough, God gave him a raise—his hourly wage increased by over 50 percent! It was a substantial raise, but Dave kept his word and gave what he had promised. Little did he know at the time that he was learning to sow bountifully. In the months that followed, he prepared to attend Bible college; but shortly before it was time to leave for school, he had a big problem with his car that would have cost more to fix than he had paid for the car. He needed a car, but he could not afford to buy one. Because he had sown bountifully, God saw fit that he would reap bountifully. Out of the blue, he received a phone call; and he could not believe what he heard—"Dave, we bought you a used car to take to college." Though he did not give to get God's blessing, the Lord certainly bestowed it upon him. Seeing the Lord's abundant provision in his time of need was a lesson that stuck with him. God is faithful!

NOTES

b. Purposefully

- Consider a verse that has helped many to discern how much to give.
- "Every man according as he purposeth in his heart, *so let him give*" (2 Corinthians 9:7). The idea behind the word *purpose* is to choose one thing over another thing. In other words, we must make decisions about how we will use our money. For instance, you may look at your budget and say, "I would like to give God a little more, but I don't have any extra. Let me see where I can spend less in order to give an offering to Him." So, you decide to cut back on eating out and discover that you have an extra $50 per month to put in the offering. Or, instead of moving into a bigger home, you decide to stay in your current house and give the extra that you would have spent in mortgage payments to God.

- The truth is that we all decide how to spend our money, and by purposing (choosing) we can find ways to give more. Again, this is totally voluntary. What God may lead one person to do He may not lead another to do.
- Through prayer you can make the right choices about how to use your money. Then, once you find God's will for your giving, follow it. Every person is to give *as he purposeth in his heart*, and that includes you.
- Whether you make a commitment to God by promising a certain percentage of your income or a set amount for faith promise missions, endeavor to keep that commitment. We should not spend our money selfishly when we have made a pledge to God. Stay true to your purpose, and God will bless you for it.

c. Willingly

- On the heels of making a commitment to God concerning our giving, we come to the phrase, "not grudgingly, or of necessity." We should never begrudge our decision to give sacrificially to God.
- When things get tight financially, we may be tempted to say, "Why did I promise to give God so much?" Though God may test our faith, we must not lose our willing spirit. Just as Abraham believed God could have raised up Isaac if he had offered him upon the altar, we must believe that God is able to supply our need after we have sacrificed for Him.
- Much can be said about a person's spiritual temperature by his reaction to the sight of the offering plate. How do you give? Do you give because you are expected to or because you do not want to look bad to those sitting near you when the plate is passed? Once again, we must think of the example of the poor Macedonian believers—*they were willing*. Oh for the grace to have that same spirit in our giving!

d. Cheerfully

- Do you want to experience God's love? Notice who He loves—"God loveth a cheerful giver" (2 Corinthians 9:7). The Greek word for *cheerful* is "hilaros." That word should look somewhat familiar because it is related to the word "hilarious." When you give out of

NOTES

love to the Lord, He will bestow more of His love and blessings upon you. That is the teaching of this verse.

- Giving with a happy heart is made possible by love.
- Illustration – Most children like to do special things for their parents. Dave Olson recalls, "I remember one particular occasion in which our children sacrificed some of their own money to buy some nice gifts for our wedding anniversary. To see the joy on their faces as they watched us open the presents was touching. They gave to us with a cheerful heart because they loved us, and we could see that love written all over their faces."
- Certainly, we have all experienced great joy by giving something special to one we love. What does it say when we don't have that same great joy when we give to God? Perhaps we do not love Him as much as we think.

NOTES

e. Sacrificially

- A sacrifice always involves a loss. When a Christian sacrifices to God, he willingly parts with things that are of value in order to please the Lord.
- The Scriptures are filled with examples of believers who made great sacrifices to God. For example: Abraham offered his son; the widow who cast her two mites into the treasury gave her all; Mary of Bethany sacrificed precious ointment that was valued at nearly a year's salary; and Barnabas sold a piece of property and gave the money to God. In every case, the Lord rewarded each of them. Sadly, many Christians never experience the blessings and joy associated with giving so sacrificially.
- The greatest of all sacrifices was made by the Lord Jesus Who "loved us, and hath given himself for us an offering and a sacrifice to God for a sweetsmelling savour" (Ephesians 5:2). Notice a couple of practical lessons we can learn from His sacrifice. ***First, sacrifices are to be made to God, not man.*** Though many have benefited from Christ's offering, He gave Himself as *a sacrifice to God.* Our motivation for giving should be to demonstrate our love for the Lord, not to impress our fellow man. ***Second, sacrifices are pleasing to the Lord.*** What Jesus did for His Father was considered *a sweetsmelling savour.* True sacrifice is like the sweet fragrance produced by incense and brings great delight to the Lord.

NOTES

- The believers in Philippi provide another wonderful picture of sacrifice. After they had given to help spread the gospel, Paul said that their gift was "an odour of a sweet smell, a sacrifice acceptable, wellpleasing to God" (Philippians 4:18). Like the offering made by Jesus, theirs was a *sweet smell* that was *wellpleasing to God.*
- If you ever want to show your love to the Lord in a special way, learn to be sacrificial in your giving. Though sacrifice incurs loss, it always benefits those for whom the sacrifice was made; and in the end, the one making the sacrifice is also blessed. What appears to be a loss is actually a win-win situation!
- Be prepared, though, to be misunderstood by others when you offer a sizeable sacrifice. When Mary anointed Jesus with the ointment, some people were upset. "And there were some that had indignation within themselves, and said, Why was this waste of the ointment made?" (Mark 14:4). What others called a *waste*, Jesus called "a good work" (Mark 14:6). Thankfully, what counts most is God's opinion!

f. Consistently

- We should be faithful in our giving. As God gives to us, we are to give to Him.
- "Honour the LORD with thy substance, and with the firstfruits of all thine increase: So shall thy barns be filled with plenty, and thy presses shall burst out with new wine" (Proverbs 3:9-10). Every time He provides a financial blessing, we are to give a portion of it back to Him. By honoring Him with our substance, we discover that He meets our needs. The words *filled with plenty* give us great hope that our faithfulness will be rewarded. Notice also that we are to give *the firstfruits.* Simply put, God gets His share first. To honor Him, you should figure your tithe before any taxes or other deductions are removed from your check. To calculate the tithe properly, give 10 percent of your gross pay, not your net pay. God should get His portion before the government!
- Part of being faithful in our giving is to give to God without delay. Paul instructed the church at Corinth, "Upon the first *day* of the week let every one of you lay by him in store, as *God* hath prospered him, that there be

no gatherings when I come" (1 Corinthians 16:2). Bring your offering to the church on the first day of the week. If you get paid on Friday, bring your tithe on Sunday. Do not wait.

- When people get tight financially, they are tempted to say, "I need the money this week, but I will make up for it next week by putting double in the offering." That is a dangerous practice. In many cases, people never double up like they plan and end up stealing from God.
- Following the Lord's simple plan of bringing your offering on the first day of the week solves the problem. Besides, God never gave us permission to borrow His money.
- Give your tithe and trust Him to meet your other needs. Be consistent in your giving.

NOTES

4. Where Are We to Give?

- Christians are supposed to be generous people, and there are no shortages of opportunities to give.
- The Hebrew Christians were told to distribute a portion of their substance—"But to do good and to communicate forget not: for with such sacrifices God is well pleased" (Hebrews 13:16).
- In Galatians 2:10, Paul spoke of his responsibility to "remember the poor." Furthermore, the apostle John spoke about assisting fellow believers—"But whoso hath this world's good, and seeth his brother have need, and shutteth up his bowels *of compassion* from him, how dwelleth the love of God in him? My little children, let us not love in word, neither in tongue; but in deed and in truth" (1 John 3:17-18). Clearly, the Lord wants us to give to the needy, but that is not to be considered our tithe.
- God's money should be brought to God's house. The Old Testament saints were instructed, "Bring ye all the tithes into the storehouse, that there may be meat in mine house" (Malachi 3:10). God defined the storehouse as His house. In our day, the local church is the storehouse. Paul instructed the church of Corinth to bring their offerings to church on the first day of the week—"Upon the first *day* of the week let every one of you lay by him in store, as *God* hath prospered him, that there be no gatherings when I come" (1 Corinthians 16:2).

- Since the tithe is to be given to the local church, it should not be sent to various Christian ministries. Remember, the tithe is the Lord's, and it is to be brought to His house.
- If you support missionaries, a radio ministry, or Christian television programming with your tithe, you have not truly tithed. You are not forbidden to give gifts to noble causes, but you should not use your tithe to do so.
- Tithes and offerings are to be brought to God's storehouse—the local church.

---

[2] Walter B. Knight, *Knight's Treasury of 2,000 Illustrations* (Grand Rapids: William B. Eerdmans Publishing Company, 1963), 140.

Review Questions

1. What two groups of people should give? the rich and poor
2. Is it a sin to be rich? Explain why or why not. No. The Bible does not condemn wealth. Many faithful Biblical characters were rich.
3. What three things should believers give? self, tithe, offering
4. Summarize how we should give. bountifully, purposefully, willingly, cheerfully, sacrificially, consistently
5. Where should tithes and offerings be brought? the local church (the storehouse)

Notes

CHAPTER FOUR

GIVE TO GOD (PART 2: OUR MOTIVATION)

Key Verse: *"Honour the LORD with thy substance, and with the firstfruits of all thine increase: So shall thy barns be filled with plenty"* (Proverbs 3:9-10).

Introductory Thoughts:

- In the last chapter, we learned God's prescribed method for giving.
- Now we will focus on our motivation to follow those instructions.
- The above passage combines the "how" and "why" aspects of giving.
- Notice that when you meet the Lord's conditions, a wonderful result occurs. By giving the *firstfruits of all thine increase,* your garners will be *filled with plenty.*
- It is simple; honor God by giving to Him, and He will bestow more blessings upon you.

1. WHY ARE WE TO GIVE?

- After all that God has done for us, it seems odd that we would have to list reasons that we should give to Him.
- Giving should flow naturally from a thankful heart, and this reveals the problem—we often do not have a spirit of gratitude.
- As we consider a few reasons for giving, hopefully, it will rekindle a heart of devotion to God and renew your motivation to give.
- So, why should we give?

NOTES

a. God Commands Us to Give

- Earlier we examined several verses regarding God's instructions about giving. He has told us who should give, what should be given, how it should be given, and where it should be given.
- His instructions are not suggestions but commands. As Master, He has the right to direct us. As Father, He knows what is best for us. As Creator, He has a design for giving. As Friend, He seeks to help us.
- If for no other reason, we should give because God told us to give. As a child, I did not understand why I should not play in the street, but I did understand that my parents did not want me to do it. As time passed, I grew to understand why. The same principle works with obeying God. Even if you do not fully comprehend why He commands a thing, your obedience will preserve your relationship with the Lord and eventually bring you into a deeper understanding of His will.
- Because God loves us, He would never require something of us that is not in our best interest. We must not have the idea that God is a mean tyrant in heaven, ruling us with a whip and delighting in making us miserable.
- As we will see, God has some great reasons for us to give.

b. Giving Demonstrates Our Love for God

- While challenging the Corinthian believers about their need to give, Paul said, "I speak . . . to prove the sincerity of your love" (2 Corinthians 8:8). Let's consider the key words in this verse.

1) The word *prove* means "to test."
    - A true test of our love for God is found in our giving. People say that they love God; but if their giving were examined, there would be little proof. Amy Carmichael, the famous missionary to India, said, "You can give without loving. But you cannot love without giving." Make sure that you give to God because you love Him, not merely because it is your duty. It may be possible that you do not love the Lord as much as you think you do.

NOTES

2) The word *sincerity* refers to genuineness.
   - Nearly every church has people who throw a little money in the offering plate so they look like real givers, but that demonstrates more love for self than for God.

3) The word *love* is the same word used to describe God's sacrificial love toward us.
   - "But God commendeth his love toward us, in that, while we were yet sinners, Christ died for us" (Romans 5:8).
   - Love that is true and genuine is willing to sacrifice by giving what is precious. By giving us His beloved Son, God demonstrated His love toward us; and as we part with things that are dear to us, we show our love and affection to Him.

➢ What a blessing to have a way to demonstrate our love to the Lord! When is the last time you gave to Him just because you wanted to please Him? Do we not express our love in a similar manner in other relationships? Of course we do. Why? We love one another and seek opportunities to display that love. Giving can be a wonderful expression of love. Let's be sure that our giving to God conveys genuine love.

➢ Paul warned about trying to give without love, saying, "And though I bestow all my goods to feed *the poor*, and though I give my body to be burned, and have not charity, it profiteth me nothing" (1 Corinthians 13:3).

➢ Too many Christians give grudgingly to God, but it is all for nothing. How sad!

c. The Lord Watches Our Giving

- Illustration – A preacher told of an experience he had while visiting another church. When the offering plates were passed, the pastor of the church walked down from the platform and stood at the end of each pew, examining what people put into the plate. At the conclusion of the service, the pastor asked the visiting preacher if there was anything he had noticed during the service that could be improved upon. Not wanting to hurt the man's feelings, the guest politely declined to comment; but the pastor pressed him saying, "Really, is there anything you

NOTES

observed that was out of the ordinary." Reluctantly, the preacher brought up the manner in which the church collected its offering. The pastor became defensive and responded, "We take our offering the Biblical way. Jesus watched how the people gave, didn't He?"
The visiting preacher replied, "Yes, but you are not Jesus." The pastor of the church had missed the important lessons of Christ's actions at the treasury and drew a wrong application from Scripture.

- Let's consider the account recorded in Mark 12:41-44 and learn a few practical principles:

"And Jesus sat over against the treasury, and beheld how the people cast money into the treasury: and many that were rich cast in much. And there came a certain poor widow, and she threw in two mites, which make a farthing. And he called unto him his disciples, and saith unto them, Verily I say unto you, That this poor widow hath cast more in, than all they which have cast into the treasury: For all they did cast in of their abundance; but she of her want did cast in all that she had, even all her living."

1) He watches who gives.
    - Jesus watched *who* gave. He knows if we truly give or not.
2) He watches how people give.
    - Our Lord also observed *how* the people gave. He knows our true motivation and attitude each time we give.
3) He sees what is given.
    - Next, Jesus saw *what* was given. The rich men gave merely of their abundance, but the poor widow gave *all her living.*
    - Although the rich people *cast in much* and the widow gave a meager two mites, Jesus said that she *cast more in.* The woman was commended not only for what she had given but because she had given *of her want,* meaning that she gave in a time of great personal need.
    - Though this passage does not teach that we should give all of our money to God, it does indicate that

NOTES

God notices not only what we give but how much we have remaining after we have given.

- Sacrifice is not measured by the size of the gift but by the size of the portion remaining. George Mueller put it this way, "God judges what we give by what we keep."[3]
- Because Jesus still watches our giving, it ought to motivate us to give sacrificially.

d. Giving Brings Joy

- Many principles of the Bible are contrary to conventional thinking. For instance, Jesus said, "It is more blessed to give than to receive" (Acts 20:35).
- The majority of people in our society focus on what they can get rather than on what they can give. This philosophy creeps into the thinking of many of us, causing us to think that we would be happier if we had a little more money, a newer car, or a bigger house. Even our prayer lives often reflect the "get" rather than "give" mentality.
- When we focus on ourselves, we become miserable.
- Illustration – Dave Olson recalls, "As a missionary, I noticed that one of the churches we led had become very self-serving. So, I decided that all the offerings that we collected during one particular December would be given to a missions project. As we challenged the members to think of others, many began to give sacrificially. This was exemplified by one of the teens in our church. Though his mother had recently died, he was determined to find money to give. With younger siblings and a drunkard for a father, there was little to spare; but he found a way to contribute. The offering time at our church became a happy occasion as people eagerly gave to help others hear the gospel in a distant nation. We had set a goal of raising $100, but the people surpassed our expectations and gave $192. For a small church consisting of poor people by our standards, this was a huge amount. Our people were thrilled that they had raised enough money to purchase 1,500 salvation Bible studies. It was the happiest December they had ever experienced. Why? *It is more blessed to give than to receive.*"

NOTES

- If you give strictly out of duty, you are missing one of the greatest benefits of giving. Once we experience the joy of giving, it will occupy our thoughts more than receiving. Surely we think about how to *give* more than how to *get* more.

e. God Gives Back

- God promises to meet the needs of those who give.
- Consider the promise made to people in the church of Philippi who gave to God's work: "But my God shall supply all your need according to his riches in glory by Christ Jesus" (Philippians 4:19). While many like to claim this verse when they have financial trouble, the promise is only for those who are givers. Earlier in the chapter, Paul noted that the people had sacrificed for the Lord's work; and because they had given, God promised to give to them and meet all of their needs.
- What a blessing to know that if I give to God, He will meet my needs!
- The Lord has a way of giving back to us even more than we give. "Give, and it shall be given unto you; good measure, pressed down, and shaken together, and running over, shall men give into your bosom. For with the same measure that ye mete withal it shall be measured to you again" (Luke 6:38). When He loads your basket, He presses it down to make more room and then adds more until it finally overflows!
- We are not to give in order to get, but we will receive tremendous blessings when we do give to God. "There is that scattereth, and yet increaseth; and *there is* that withholdeth more than is meet, but *it tendeth* to poverty" (Proverbs 11:24). When we are generous, we are entrusted with more; and when we are stingy, we suffer loss.
- <u>Illustration</u> – Dave Olson shared an example of God's provision in his life. He said, "Shortly after we returned from the mission field, our church held its annual stewardship banquet. Each year, the members of our church pray and ask God to show how much they should give for the upcoming fiscal year. I was unsure how much I could work because my health had drastically declined while living in Africa. At the time, we were

NOTES

still receiving monthly support from several churches, but I knew much of that support would drop. God clearly challenged me to give a certain amount, and for the next four months we managed just fine. At the beginning of the year, our income dramatically plummeted. After giving God what we had promised and paying our health insurance, we only had $54 to carry us through until the next month's paycheck. My wife and I knew that it was right to keep our promise to God and found ourselves looking to Him to keep His promise to us.[4] After all, He had said, 'Give, and it shall be given unto you.' I wish could say that I had tremendous faith. My attitude was more like the man who approached Jesus saying, 'Lord, I believe; help thou mine unbelief' (Mark 9:24). Thankfully, our Savior is faithful. Within a week or so, I received a check in the mail for $1,200! When I got home and showed my wife, tears of joy filled her eyes. We knew that God was still with us and was going to take care of us. Though we lost so much of our expected income, God made up for it throughout the entire year in ways we never would have imagined. By the time the next stewardship banquet rolled around, God had not only enabled us to give what we promised but also met all of our needs in the process. Though I do not give to get, I have been amazed at how much I get when I give faithfully to God."

NOTES

f. Your Giving Determines if Souls Go to Heaven or Hell

- It is very sobering to consider that if ministries are not properly funded, people will not hear the gospel. Let's face it, it takes money to print tracts, run Sunday School buses, have a VBS, buy Bibles, and send missionaries to foreign lands. Let's consider a couple examples.
- Example – Any church that runs a Sunday School bus knows how expensive it can be. The cost of the bus, insurance, repairs, and fuel can really add up. However, those involved in the bus ministry also know the tremendous joy it brings to see a family reached with the gospel. It is worth every penny spent! How could you put a price tag on the souls of boys and girls? How could it be too expensive to reach people in your community?

Praise God for those who care enough to run buses through their neighborhoods! While there is no command in the Bible to run buses, it is an effective way to touch lives with the gospel.

- Illustration – When Dave Olson's wife Lisa was a little girl, she started going to church on a bus. What if members of that church were not willing to give to keep that bus running? She and her family would not be saved, she never would have gone to the mission field, and the souls that she has led to Christ never would have been reached. The area of giving to missions is close to the Olsons' hearts because they have seen firsthand how lives in distant lands are affected by giving.
- Illustration – Dave Olson recalls, "Several people with whom we have shared the gospel have already entered into eternity; and if we had not gotten to the mission field, they would be in hell today. When my family arrived on the mission field, the life expectancy of the average Zambian was only 35 years old. Many people die before that age. Consider the story of a boy named Loy. The following is an excerpt from a prayer letter dated June 23, 2003:

> We are reminded over and over again of the mercies of God. There was a thirteen-year-old boy coming to church for the past several months named Loy. One day Lisa was out soulwinning and came across Loy. He started speaking to her in the tribal language. At that time, my wife could only recognize one word—Bible. At first, she thought he was asking for a Bible as so many people do. The lady she was soulwinning with translated what he really said. He was asking them to come to his house so they could teach him the Bible. Of course, they went and witnessed to him and his mother. Both prayed to receive Christ.
>
> Loy became very faithful to church and always had a sweet spirit about him. My wife always commented about how different Loy was compared to the other children that came to church. A couple of months ago, we held a baptism service, and Loy wanted to be baptized. He had questions about his salvation, and we made sure that he was truly saved. He was the most excited one being baptized that day.
>
> Last month, Loy got sick and less than a week later he died. Normally, I do not enjoy preaching at funerals, but it was much easier to preach this time because of his testimony. About two hundred people from town came,

NOTES

> and they got to hear a clear salvation message. The next Sunday, we had more people in church because of the funeral.
>
> We are so happy to be here for people like Loy. So many times we reach them just before they die. Thank you for making it possible for us to be here to win these lost people.

That prayer letter was written only a year after we reached the mission field. What I did not tell you was that we had raised our support to go to the mission field in just 16 months. Had we been on deputation like many families for two or three years, Loy could have been dead long before we arrived. I am glad that people in churches saw the need to give to the cause of missions and sent us to the field in a timely manner. I'm sure that Loy is glad, too."

- Illustration – Dave Olson provided another story. "Mr. Phiri lived in the little town of Pemba. He was a frail man dwelling in a small home with a grass-thatched roof. One Thursday, a man from our church wanted me to go with him to tell Mr. Phiri about Christ. When we arrived at the house, we exchanged the customary greetings and sat outside on small stools. Then I began to explain how Jesus died for his sins. Mr. Phiri was a nominal Muslim, but that day he put his faith in the Lord Jesus Christ. A couple of days after his salvation, Mr. Phiri entered the clinic due to failing health. Many people with tuberculosis also suffer from AIDS, and it is probable that he suffered from both diseases. Just days after entering the clinic, Mr. Phiri entered eternity. Oh, how grateful we are that people sacrificed so that men like Mr. Phiri could be told the truth about Jesus before dying! What if people had never given and we were never sent?"
- In 3 John 5-8, the apostle commended the believers for their sacrifice in helping those who were carrying the truth to the regions beyond. By assisting those missionaries, they had become "fellowhelpers to the truth." Not everybody can go to the mission field, but we can all help those who are sent. In fact, the apostle said that we "ought to." Will you?

NOTES

- When a church holds a missions conference to determine how much it will raise for missionaries, it is more like a business meeting to determine the fate of the unsaved. When God's people fail to give as they ought, the Good News is carried to fewer people. On the other hand, when many believers sacrifice and give a little extra, it adds up to a lot.
- One of the most important reasons to give is so that other people can be saved. Have you ever stopped to realize that the eternal destiny of others may hinge on your giving? Could you give more to reach souls? Perhaps we should be challenged by the words of the famous hymn, "By and by when I look on His face, I'll wish I had given Him more."

NOTES

2. What Hinders Giving?

- Since giving is so important, it is wise to consider things that might hinder us from giving and remove those hindrances from our lives.

a. Selfishness

- On top of the list is self. It is not wrong to spend money for personal needs. However, it is easy to become self-centered, especially since we are constantly bombarded by advertising which tells us that their product is the solution to all of our problems. It is amazing how quickly we spend money on items that promise to make our lives more comfortable. Keep in mind that a decision to buy something for self is also a decision to have less for God and others.
- Jesus warned about the "me first" mentality in the Gospels. He even gave a parable about a rich man who spent all of his money on accumulating more things for himself. "But God said unto him, *Thou* fool," and Jesus added, "So *is* he that layeth up treasure for himself, and is not rich toward God" (Luke 12:20-21).
- It is foolish to heap up treasures and possessions for ourselves and neglect God.

b. Lack of a Budget

- Any Christian right with God wants to give to the Lord. However, those who never learn to budget their money will be hindered in their giving. I know many people with big hearts who willingly sacrifice for others. However, because they do not manage their money properly, they get into financial trouble. They wrongly assume that because they have given to God that He is obligated to get them out of the mess they have created.

- Giving to God is not what creates a crisis—failing to control their spending in other areas is what brings the problems. Soon, they become frustrated because the bill collectors are after them, and they have less to give to God. Isn't it better to learn to manage your money so that you have a little extra to give to special causes when needs arise?

c. Debt

- When a person is in debt, he should still tithe and give a small offering; but he is no longer able to give generously until he gets himself out of debt. God expects us to pay our debts, and it is sin to borrow and not repay. For generous people, this is a hard pill to swallow. If they "follow their heart" and continue to give money that they do not have, they will go deeper into debt.
- We find no command in the Bible to go into debt in order to give. Paul told the believers in Corinth, "For if there be first a willing mind, *it is* accepted according to that a man hath, *and* not according to that he hath not" (2 Corinthians 8:12).
- We are not expected to give money that we do not have, but we are obligated to tithe on our income. If you are currently in debt, pay it off as quickly as possible; and then you will have extra to give to worthy causes.

d. Lack of Faith

- Many people know that they should tithe and give an offering to God, but they cannot see how they will make ends meet if they give. What is the problem? They lack faith. Faith looks to God instead of the circumstances.
- If you are struggling to obey God, you are not the first person. However, once you take a step of faith and obey the Lord, you will find Him to be faithful to you. "But without faith *it is* impossible to please *him*: for he that cometh to God must believe that he is, and *that* he is a rewarder of them that diligently seek him" (Hebrews 11:6).

NOTES

- Will you trust Him enough to meet your needs? If you do, you will find Him true to His Word. He has promised to take care of you.

NOTES

3. What Happens if We Fail to Give?

- Whether you fail to give because of stubbornness, covetousness, fear, or a lack of faith—the end result is still the same. You will suffer consequences for your disobedience.

a. Blessings Are Missed

- God wants to load you with blessings. Consider the wonderful promise that He gives to those who are obedient in the area of giving: "Bring ye all the tithes into the storehouse, that there may be meat in mine house, and prove me now herewith, saith the LORD of hosts, if I will not open you the windows of heaven, and pour you out a blessing, that *there shall* not *be room* enough *to receive it*" (Malachi 3:10). When God opens His windows and pours out blessings, we will have more than we need.
- When we give, we will not only have rewards in this life but also in the life to follow. Jesus said, "But lay up for yourselves treasures in heaven, where neither moth nor rust doth corrupt, and where thieves do not break through nor steal" (Matthew 6:20). Giving to God results in heavenly treasures which cannot lose their value.
- Illustration – One man had the following words inscribed on his tombstone, "What I spent, I lost. What I saved, I left. What I gave, I have." That is the right perspective to have regarding our money. However, when we don't give, we forfeit many blessings here and in the hereafter.

b. A Curse Is Given

- Failing to give to God creates financial problems.
- The Lord revealed to His people that stealing the tithe led to a curse on their finances. "Ye *are* cursed with a curse: for ye have robbed me, *even* this whole nation" (Malachi 3:9). In fact, the curse was in the form of "the devourer," which destroyed their harvest (v. 11). In those days, a person's livelihood depended on a good harvest. So,

when God allowed their harvest to be spoiled, it ruined their financial situation.

- Even today, people who refuse to give God what belongs to Him may fall under a financial curse. Some say, "I can't afford to give anything to God." The truth is that you can't afford not to give! As a Christian, you should never expect financial blessings until you follow God's plan of giving. Thankfully, once you begin to give, God will lift the curse. Consider what He told His people would happen after they began to give: "And I will rebuke the devourer for your sakes, and he shall not destroy the fruits of your ground; neither shall your vine cast her fruit before the time in the field, saith the LORD of hosts" (Malachi 3:11).
- Could some of your financial strains be the result of robbing God? If so, start giving and ask God to rebuke *the devourer.*
- God's Word often describes our condition to a tee. Haggai 1:6-7 reads, "Ye have sown much, and bring in little; ye eat, but ye have not enough; ye drink, but ye are not filled with drink; ye clothe you, but there is none warm; and he that earneth wages earneth wages *to put it* into a bag with holes. Thus saith the LORD of hosts; Consider your ways." Do the phrases *bring in little* and *have not enough* describe your life? Does it seem as if your money is being put into a *bag with holes*? If so, please realize that you cannot resist God and still expect a bountiful life.
- If you are one of His children and fail to give, you will suffer the consequences. It is not because God takes pleasure in seeing you suffer but because He wants to load you with blessings for being obedient. It is your choice—a blessing or a curse. Which will you choose?

NOTES

Review Questions

1. According to Proverbs 3:9-10, givers are promised to be *"filled with plenty."*
2. Summarize why we should give to God. God commands us, it demonstrates our love for God, the Lord watches our giving, it brings joy, God gives back, it determines if souls will be saved
3. What four things can hinder our giving? selfishness, lack of a budget, debt, lack of faith
4. What could you do to rid yourself of the hindrances stated above? answers will vary
5. When we fail to give as we should, what happens to us? blessings are missed, a curse is given

---

[3] Knight, *Knight's Treasury of 2,000 Illustrations,* 139.

[4] In most situations, when a person's income is drastically reduced, his tithe and offering is also adjusted. Since we had made a promise to God about our giving, we believed we should keep our promise. God does not command Christians to promise a certain amount of offering every week, month, or year. However, at times, He may lead believers to make promises about their giving, and such promises should not be made lightly. "When thou shalt vow a vow unto the LORD thy God, thou shalt not slack to pay it" (Deuteronomy 23:21).

CHAPTER FIVE

HELP OTHERS

Key Verse: *"The righteous considereth the cause of the poor: but the wicked regardeth not to know it"* (Proverbs 29:7).

Introductory Thoughts:

- Selfish people never find lasting satisfaction because their hands cling to their treasure. What they fail to realize is that in order to reach for happiness, they must open their hands and let go of some of what they have. It is only as we extend a hand to the needy that we will grasp true joy.
- Winston Churchill said, "We make a living by what we get, but we make a life by what we give."[5] Truly, your life is a reflection of your giving.
- Much can be determined about a man's character by observing how he treats the poor and needy.
- A good man thinks of others, not just himself; and a wicked man disregards the needs of the poor. Though we are responsible to help others in their times of affliction, we should not confuse this with our obligation to God.
- The tithe belongs to the Lord and should be brought to the local church. However, as we shall see, there are rewards for being generous to our fellow men.

1. WHO SHOULD WE HELP?

- Some people are very generous and try to help with any need that comes to their attention. It is not possible to give to every noble cause, but we should be willing.
- As we are led by God's Spirit, He will guide us to make the right decisions about who to assist.
- In the Word of God, we have further guidance to help us know who we are obligated to help.

NOTES

a. The Poor

NOTES

- The phrase *the poor* is found in Scripture over 130 times, and God repeatedly urges us to consider their plight.
- While some successful people despise the poor, thinking that they are poor due to laziness and a lack of character, they are often mistaken. Some families fall upon hard times because of circumstances beyond their control such as health problems, the loss of the father, or a lack of education.
- Many poor people simply lack the opportunities that other hardworking people are afforded, and with a little assistance they can be on the road to changing their situation.
- The Lord does not want us to have a hard heart toward the poor.
- "If there be among you a poor man of one of thy brethren . . . thou shalt not harden thine heart, nor shut thine hand from thy poor brother" (Deuteronomy 15:7). Notice the connection between the heart and the hand. Our giving is directly tied to our heart's attitude.
- Instead of ignoring those suffering hardship, we ought to have compassion. "He that hath pity upon the poor lendeth unto the LORD" (Proverbs 19:17).
- If we are truly spiritual, we will at least consider the needs of others. "The righteous considereth the cause of the poor" (Proverbs 29:7).
- Instead of looking the other way when we notice someone's difficulty, let us at least prayerfully consider what God would have us to do. When we do, we may find ourselves emulating the kindness of the virtuous woman—*"She stretcheth out her hand to the poor; yea, she reacheth forth her hands to the needy"* (Proverbs 31:20).
- Sadly, in this age of entitlement, some people refuse to work. They depend upon the government and squander what they have.
- Paul told the church in Thessalonica, "For even when we were with you, this we commanded you, that if any would not work, neither should he eat" (2 Thessalonians 3:10). Because the Scriptures clearly command that able-bodied men should work to support their family, we are

not necessarily required to help poor people who refuse to work.

NOTES

b. The Afflicted

- The judges in Asaph's day were reminded of their duty—"Defend the poor and fatherless: do justice to the afflicted and needy" (Psalm 82:3).
- God has a special place in His heart for the afflicted. Notice His particular concern for the fatherless and widows. "A father of the fatherless, and a judge of the widows, *is* God in his holy habitation" (Psalm 68:5).
- To be godly, we must maintain a watchful eye over those who cannot care for themselves. Did not Elisha relieve the widow and her two sons?

c. Fellow Christians

- While we should be willing to help all people, we must make our care for the brethren a top priority. "As we have therefore opportunity, let us do good unto all *men*, especially unto them who are of the household of faith" (Galatians 6:10).
- As David provided for Mephibosheth for Jonathan's sake, we should care for fellow Christians because they are God's children. While detailing activities in which believers should be engaged, Paul included, "Distributing to the necessity of saints" (Romans 12:13).
- Not only should we give to those brethren who are prominent in the church but to those who are less able to repay our kindness.
- Jesus spoke about those who will be rewarded during the judgment, saying, "Verily I say unto you, Inasmuch as ye have done *it* unto one of the least of these my brethren, ye have done *it* unto me" (Matthew 25:40). Notice that the acts of kindness were displayed to *the least of these my brethren.* Be willing to help any of God's people.

d. Those Whom God Puts in Your Path

- God may want to use you to demonstrate His love to the unsaved by helping them in their affliction. A great example of this is the Good Samaritan. The man who fell among thieves was neglected by the religious men who encountered him, but the Good Samaritan "went to *him*, and bound up his wounds, pouring in oil and wine, and set him on his own beast and brought him to an inn, and took care of him" (Luke 10:34). The Good Samaritan is called good because he was willing to share his substance and money to care for a suffering man. At the end of the parable, Jesus said, "Go, and do thou likewise" (v. 37), leaving us with instructions to be considerate of the needy. Sometimes the needs of others are greater than our own, and it would be wrong not to help.

- Illustration – Dave Olson gives the following testimony: "While living in Zambia, I recall approaching a humble, helpless crippled man as I walked down the busy sidewalk. His emaciated body found little comfort on the hard pavement where he sat for hours looking for alms from those who passed his way. Though he never asked me for anything, I felt compelled to buy him a hot meal and a cool drink. When I returned with the food, his eyes widened and a warm smile expressed true gratitude. He was overwhelmed that I went out of my way to get him something to eat instead of just giving him a small amount of money. When I handed him a gospel tract, the message was already backed up by a deed that supported the message in the tract. You do not have to live in Africa to have opportunities to help others."
- You can bring a meal to a sick neighbor, buy some lemonade from the kid at the end of the street, help someone with a flat tire, assist the lady in front of you at the checkout line when she is short a couple of dollars, etc.
- In many cases, we are so concerned about ourselves that we miss opportunities to be a witness to others. If God puts someone in your path this week, remember to be a Good Samaritan.

2. How Can We Help Others?

- Now that we know we are to help others, let's consider how to do so in a manner pleasing to God. Here are a couple of principles to follow.

NOTES

a. Give Readily

- One of the biggest obstacles to overcome in giving to others is selfishness. Therefore, we must prepare our heart to be generous and in a state of readiness.
- Paul told Timothy to charge those who were financially able to be "ready to distribute, willing to communicate" (1 Timothy 6:18). The word *communicate* means "to impart or give to another."
- When we have been blessed materially, God expects us to be ready and willing to part with some of those blessings.

b. Give Generously

- Let us consider the giving of the Macedonian believers once again: "How that in a great trial of affliction the abundance of their joy and their deep poverty abounded unto the riches of their liberality" (2 Corinthians 8:2). Despite being poor, they abounded in generosity. Although we use the example of these believers to teach principles about giving to God, we must remember that the context of the passage shows that they were actually giving to other Christians in need—"Praying us with much intreaty that we would receive the gift, and *take upon us* the fellowship of the ministering to the saints" (2 Corinthians 8:4). Because they had already given themselves to God, they were willing to sacrifice for His children.
- Perhaps the reason we fail to give generously is because we have not truly given ourselves to God.

c. Give Honorably

- Our purpose in giving to others should not be to earn a name for ourselves.
- Many wealthy people donate money to charity to get publicity for themselves. In Jesus' day, the Pharisees sounded a trumpet to draw attention to their good works. However, Jesus instructed, "But when thou doest alms, let not thy left hand know what thy right hand doeth: That thine alms may be in secret: and thy Father which seeth in secret himself shall reward thee openly" (Matthew 6:3-4). Alms refers to giving something to relieve the poor.
- In most cases, the people you assist will know what you have done; but you are not to publicize your good works

NOTES

to be respected by others. Give to glorify the Lord, and He will reward you.

NOTES

d. Give Thoughtfully

- Charles Haddon Spurgeon said, "Many give their money to the poor in a hurry, without thought; and many more give nothing at all."[6] True concern requires thoughtful consideration.
- In Proverbs 29:7, Solomon taught, "The righteous considereth the cause of the poor." His father, David, expressed the same idea, "Blessed *is* he that considereth the poor: the LORD will deliver him in time of trouble" (Psalm 41:1). Spurgeon explains, "This precious promise belongs to those who *'consider'* the poor, look into their case, devise plans for their benefit, and considerately carry them out. We can do more by care than by cash, and most with the two together."[7] Taking time to think how you can be a blessing to others is just as important as the gift you bestow.
- Men like George Mueller and Charles Spurgeon were thoughtful about giving to others. They built orphanages and provided meals, medical care, clothing, and education for thousands of children. Some may call it a social gospel, but they believed it was part of Christianity.
- What can you and your church do to fulfill your duty to consider the cause of the poor?

e. Give Carefully

- Much has been said already about the need to give, but we must include a word of caution. Though we must be generous, we must also exercise discretion.
- "A good man sheweth favour, and lendeth: he will guide his affairs with discretion" (Psalm 112:5). This verse teaches that the head must be involved as well as the heart. When done wisely, giving will be to the right person for the right reason at the right time with the right resources. If you give to every need you encounter, you will go broke. Part of being a *good man* as mentioned in the verse is to be careful in our almsgiving.

- Never go into debt in order to give. You must not risk future opportunities to help others because of careless stewardship.

3. Why Should We Help Others?

- The number of reasons to help others abounds. In addition to what we have already considered, think about the following:

a. Helping Others Is Commanded

- When the children of Israel were about to enter the Promised Land, God reminded them how He wanted them to act.
- Even during the dispensation of the Law, God demonstrated compassion to the unfortunate, saying, "For the poor shall never cease out of the land: therefore I command thee, saying, Thou shalt open thine hand wide unto thy brother, to thy poor, and to thy needy, in thy land" (Deuteronomy 15:11). Notice the clarity of the words, *I command thee.* Further, God said, "Thou shalt," leaving no doubt what His will is for His people.
- Instead of clasping tightly to our substance, we are to open our hand wide and relieve those in need.
- God often blesses people with much so that they can be a blessing to others. John the Baptist preached, "He that hath two coats, let him impart to him that hath none" (Luke 3:11). It could be that God has given you extra to share with someone who is lacking.

b. Helping Others Demonstrates the Love of God

- Twelve times the phrase *love one another* is found in the New Testament. As we have already seen, we cannot love without giving.
- The apostle John conveyed this truth well when he said, "But whoso hath this world's good, and seeth his brother have need, and shutteth up his bowels *of compassion* from him, how dwelleth the love of God in him? My little children, let us not love in word, neither in tongue; but in deed and in truth" (1 John 3:17-18). Love is measured more by action than by words. When a fellow believer is truly destitute, the love of God motivates us to do something. Among Christians, a need should lead to a deed.

NOTES

- Illustration – Dave Olson said, "I learned much about love and giving by observing believers in our ministry in Zambia. A particularly poor family in our congregation was very generous. On one occasion, despite not having much for themselves, they gave to a new lady in our church who was struggling to provide food for her family. How could they give so sacrificially? The love of God constrained them. Shouldn't it constrain us, too?"

NOTES

c. Helping Others Secures Blessings

- Those who give to others do not lose anything in the end. In fact, it is considered a loan to God that will be repaid in due time.
- "He that hath pity upon the poor lendeth unto the LORD; and that which he hath given will he pay him again." (Proverbs 19:17). Relieving the poor is the safest loan you can ever make because it is backed by the bank of heaven. Not only are we recompensed in this life, we have the promise of eternal rewards.
- Jesus preached, "Sell that ye have, and give alms; provide yourselves bags which wax not old, a treasure in the heavens that faileth not, where no thief approacheth, neither moth corrupteth" (Luke 12:33). By parting with this world's goods and giving to the needy, we can secure treasures in heaven that will never fade away.
- Our gift does not have to be large to be noticed by God. Jesus said, "For whosoever shall give you a cup of water to drink in my name, because ye belong to Christ, verily I say unto you, he shall not lose his reward" (Mark 9:41). Let us determine to do what we can, and leave the rest in God's hands.

d. Helping Others Guarantees Future Deliverance

- God delivers those who are considerate of the needy.
- "Blessed *is* he that considereth the poor: the LORD will deliver him in time of trouble" (Psalm 41:1).
- One day, you will have needs, and if you have taken care of others, God will take care of you. What a wonderful insurance policy is provided by our Lord to generous believers! If you consider the poor, you can boldly claim God's promise to deliver you when your day of trouble comes.

e. Helping Others Provides a Motivation to Work

- Believe it or not, your goal in working is not only to provide for your family. Through our hard work, we have the opportunity to help others suffering hardships.
- Consider Paul's testimony, "I have shewed you all things, how that so labouring ye ought to support the weak, and to remember the words of the Lord Jesus, how he said, It is more blessed to give than to receive" (Acts 20:35). We usually quote the last part of the verse concerning the joy that we receive from giving, but we often neglect the first part which instructs us to work in order to help the weak. The *weak* include sickly and feeble people.
- Sadly, Christians have willingly relinquished the responsibility for caring for such brothers to government agencies. Though God expects people to provide for their own families, the early churches understood the importance of sharing with those who legitimately could not provide for themselves.

f. Helping Others Brings Happiness

- David realized the joy that comes from relieving the poor. He said, "Blessed *is* he that considereth the poor" (Psalm 41:1). The word *blessed* means happy. Happiness often seems elusive, but one way to secure it is to be a blessing to other people.
- If you recall, when Paul quoted Jesus saying, "It is more blessed to give than to receive," the context of the passage was dealing with giving to the weak and feeble. So, those who give to the needy are the ones who are truly promised joy.
- Consider Solomon's wisdom, "He that despiseth his neighbour sinneth: but he that hath mercy on the poor, happy *is* he" (Proverbs 14:21).

g. Helping Others Overcomes Covetousness

- We tend to be collectors, buying things just because we can. People with hobbies continually gather for their collection. Men buy tools, guns, and "big-boy toys." Women collect shoes, clothing, furniture, bells, fine china, furniture, figurines, etc. If you have a problem with coveting, try giving some of your substance away.

NOTES

- "He coveteth greedily all the day long: but the righteous giveth and spareth not" (Proverbs 21:26). This verse teaches that giving is the opposite of coveting.
- The next time you are tempted to purchase something because of covetousness, consider using that money to be a blessing to someone else. That just might cure you!

h. Helping Others Pleases God

- Our highest aim in life must be to please our Lord and Savior. Since He has done so much for us, we ought to honor Him by delighting in what He delights.
- What brings Him pleasure? "But to do good and to communicate forget not: for with such sacrifices God is well pleased" (Hebrews 13:16). The Lord considers our willingness to distribute to the needs of others as a sacrifice. Further, He is *well pleased* by those actions.
- It makes sense, therefore, that we ought to engage in what makes Him happy.

4. What if We Fail to Help Others?

- If we are unwilling to assist others in their time of need, it reveals that we have a selfish spirit. Consider a couple of the consequences of refusing to lend a hand.

a. We Will Be Neglected

- It is sobering to realize that we will be treated as we have treated others. As we saw earlier, God will give to those who have given to the needy. However, if we harden our heart and close our ears to the cry of the destitute, we guarantee hardship for ourselves.
- "Whoso stoppeth his ears at the cry of the poor, he also shall cry himself, but shall not be heard" (Proverbs 21:13). How frightful to not heard by God or by man! We cannot expect help if we refuse to give it to others.

b. We Will Be Cursed

- A curse is typically thought of as a wish for trouble to another, but it can also have another meaning. When God puts a curse on man, it is a divine judgment for disobedience. When we ignore His commands to relieve the poor, we secure a curse on our lives.

NOTES

- "He that giveth unto the poor shall not lack: but he that hideth his eyes shall have many a curse" (Proverbs 28:27). Be careful to see the needs that God wants you to see. Otherwise, you will have *many a curse.*

NOTES

Concluding Thoughts:

✓ While a chapter on helping others may not be a common feature in most books about personal finances, it is vital part of stewardship. Because God provides many blessings for assisting the needy and stern warnings for neglecting their condition, we should not take the subject lightly.

✓ Perhaps the reason so many Christians suffer financially is because they have disregarded God's clear commands to help one another.

✓ God does not expect us to give all of our money away. That would contradict several other passages of Scripture about money management. He expects us to provide for our own, save, leave an inheritance, etc. However, it is our duty to keep our eyes and ears open to needs around us, prayerfully considering which situations the Lord would have us to act upon.

✓ As we walk in obedience to God's guidance, we will secure His blessings.

Review Questions

1. According to Proverbs 29:7, what kind of person does not care to know about the needs of the poor? the wicked
2. What four groups of people are we supposed to help? the poor, the afflicted, fellow Christians, those that God puts in our path
3. Summarize how we can help others. give readily, generously, honorably, thoughtfully, carefully
4. Since we cannot give to every needy person, how can we determine who we should help? answers will vary – consider Scripture, pray, be observant
5. List four reasons why we should help others. we are commanded, it demonstrates love for God, it secures blessings, it guarantees future deliverance, it provides motivation to work, it brings happiness, it overcomes covetousness, it pleases God

---

[5] Berger, "Top 100 Money Quotes of All Time."
[6] Charles H. Spurgeon, *Faith's Checkbook* (Chicago: Moody Press, 1992), 19.
[7] Ibid.

CHAPTER SIX

LIVE RIGHT

Key Verse: *"But seek ye first the kingdom of God, and his righteousness; and all these things shall be added unto you"* (Matthew 6:33).

Introductory Thoughts:

- What most people fail to realize is that God has plainly promised to bless those who live a righteous life. This does not mean that you will become rich by being righteous, but God will meet your material needs.
- A common verse quoted when counseling people is, "But seek ye first the kingdom of God, and his righteousness; and all these things shall be added unto you" (Matthew 6:33). When God is placed first, *all these things* will be supplied; but when one seeks *all these things,* he pushes God aside and forfeits the Lord's blessings.
- Remember, "Ye cannot serve God and mammon" (Matthew 6:24).

1. CURSED OR BLESSED?

- Notice the blessing of the righteous and the curse on the wicked: "The LORD will not suffer the soul of the righteous to famish: but he casteth away the substance of the wicked" (Proverbs 10:3).
- How a person lives has a direct effect on his financial situation. For instance, many drunkards and drug addicts lose everything and end up in homeless shelters.
- While the wicked suffer loss, God delights to bless His people. David testified, "I have been young, and *now* am old; yet have I not seen the righteous forsaken, nor his seed begging bread" (Psalm 37:25).
- The Lord takes care of His own better than anyone can care for himself.

NOTES

2. Short-lived Prosperity of the Wicked

- At times we become jealous of how well others seem to fare.
- The psalmist, Asaph, wrote of a similar experience, "For I was envious at the foolish, *when* I saw the prosperity of the wicked" (Psalm 73:3).
- It is difficult to watch evil people prosper financially and amass many earthly treasures.
- Have you ever reasoned, "I'm trying to live for God, but that guy is a crook and has everything going for him. He's got a big house, a nice car, and all the latest gadgets. It's not fair"? Asaph also muttered similar words, "they have more than heart could wish" (v. 7).
- Human nature tends to see how good the other guy has it, but spiritually-minded people understand that the prosperity of the wicked is short lived. Evil people are set in "slippery places" and will be "*brought* into desolation, as in a moment!" (v. 18-19). Once they fall, there will be none to lift them up.
- On the contrary, those who live for the Lord dwell in His presence and are spared the terrible hardships reserved for the wicked.
- The psalmist acknowledged God's sustaining hand, saying, "Nevertheless I *am* continually with thee: thou hast holden *me* by my right hand" (v. 23). In the end, living right always pays off!

3. God's Guarantee

- Observe another promise, "Blessed *is* the man *that* feareth the LORD, *that* delighteth greatly in his commandments . . . Wealth and riches *shall be* in his house: and his righteousness endureth for ever" (Psalm 112:1, 3).
- Those who fear the Lord and obey His commandments will be blessed financially. Once again, we see a connection between our behavior and material blessings. People who live a wicked, backslidden life cannot claim this promise. However, when we delight in the Lord, He will delight in blessing us.
- Financial blessings do not necessarily equal lavish wealth. Don't forget the true riches we spoke of earlier.
- "Blessed *is* every one that feareth the LORD; that walketh in his ways. For thou shalt eat the labour of thine hands: happy

Notes

shalt thou *be*, and *it shall be* well with thee" (Psalm 128:1-2). According to this verse, those who fear God and walk in His ways are promised three benefits:

a. Their basic needs will be met—*thou shalt eat the labour of thine hands.*
b. They will be happy—*happy shalt thou be.* Who doesn't want to be happy?
c. They will have peace and satisfaction—*it shall be well with thee.*

- Rest assured that God will richly reward your godly lifestyle. We are promised that "the LORD will give grace and glory: no good *thing* will he withhold from them that walk uprightly" (Psalm 84:11). In return for walking uprightly, God will give you anything that is good and helpful for you. With that in mind, let's straighten up!
- In case you need more assurance of God's willingness to provide for you, consider another nugget—"He that spared not his own Son, but delivered him up for us all, how shall he not with him also freely give us all things?" (Romans 8:32). Since God has already given us His best, how could we doubt that He is inclined to *freely give us all things*?
- Thankfully, the Lord not only told us that He would take care of us but also recorded examples of His provision in the Bible. Moses reminded the Israelites of God's supply during their time in the wilderness saying, ". . . these forty years the LORD thy God *hath been* with thee; thou hast lacked nothing" (Deuteronomy 2:7). Their clothes and shoes did not wear out for four decades! The Lord is still in the same business of providing for His faithful servants. As He met the needs of the Israelites, He can provide for you, too.

CONCLUDING THOUGHTS:

✓ Never be tempted to think that a life of holiness will go unrewarded.

✓ "For God *is* not unrighteous to forget your work and labour of love, which ye have shewed toward his name, in that ye have ministered to the saints, and do minister" (Hebrews 6:10).

✓ The Lord pays the best wages imaginable. Not only are we blessed here on earth, but we also have the opportunity to lay up treasures in heaven.

NOTES

Review Questions

1. According to Matthew 6:33, what two things must we seek in order to have our needs met? the kingdom of God, God's righteousness
2. What two things cannot be served at the same time? See Matthew 6:24. God, mammon
3. According to Psalm 37:25, who will not be forsaken? the righteous
4. In Psalm 73:3, who did Asaph wrongly envy? the foolish
5. What three benefits are promised to those who fear and obey God? basic needs will be met, happiness, peace

Chapter Seven

Control Your Spending

Key Verse: *"Moreover it is required in stewards, that a man be found faithful"* (1 Corinthians 4:2).

Introductory Thoughts:

- If you do not control your money, it may soon control you.
- The best way to regulate your spending is to set up and follow a budget.
- Many people talk loosely about their "budget" but often have no idea what it means have one. For instance, when someone is asked to donate to a good cause, he responds by saying, "I'd love to, but it's not in my budget." What he means is that he doesn't want to spend money on it. However, that same person is apt to purchase something he was not planning to buy simply because the item was on sale. In reality, he does not have an organized budget. To him, if he wants it, it is in his "budget."

1. Why You Need a Budget

- The Bible sheds light on the importance of controlling our money.
- Since God is the One Who gives us what we have, it is wise to consult His Word to know how to take care of it. Consider a couple principles from the Bible.

a. Manage

- God expects you to faithfully manage what is given to you.
- "Moreover it is required in stewards, that a man be found faithful" (1 Corinthians 4:2). A *steward* is a manager, and the word *faithful* means "to be trustworthy." In other words, whatever God gives you, He expects you to manage wisely. You must not be careless or wasteful in using any of your money.

Notes

- Having a budget enables you to better manage what God has entrusted to you. Without a budget, you will find it difficult to be a good steward.
- If making a budget helps us to fulfill God's will of being faithful stewards, it makes sense for every Christian to diligently follow a budget.

b. Organize

- You must organize your spending.
- We are exhorted, "Let all things be done decently and in order" (1 Corinthians 14:40). Obviously, *"all things"* includes money!
- By establishing a budget, you arrange your financial obligations *in order* and decide where your money goes.
- You ought to diligently plan how each dollar is to be spent.
- Keeping track of your expenses is good, but planning your spending ahead of time is better.
- A budget provides a roadmap to get you where you need to be financially.

c. Count the Cost

- Each individual must learn to consider what he can and cannot afford to purchase.
- Although there are many things in life that we would like to own, we are not always able to afford them.
- As discussed earlier, overextending financially leads to debt and bondage.
- When planning to make a purchase, determine if you have enough to pay for it.
- Jesus gave an example to follow. "For which of you, intending to build a tower, sitteth not down first, and counteth the cost, whether he have *sufficient* to finish *it*?" (Luke 14:28). Learn to count the cost of your expenses to ensure that you do not make financial commitments that you cannot meet.
- Determine if you can make not only the initial payment but also the final one!

NOTES

2. Why People Don't Have Budgets

- The word *budget* is an unpleasant word in many households. The thought of making and sticking to a budget seems so restrictive. After all, who wants to be put in a box or forced to follow an uncomfortable way of life?
- Unfortunately, those without a budget fail to realize that controlling their money can be quite liberating.
- The truth is that people who overspend end up in bondage, not those who have their spending under control.
- Hearing the word *budget* stirs up guilt in the conscience of people who know that they ought to tame their spending practices.
- Consequently, out of self-defense, they begin to make excuses why they are not ready to have a budget. Let's consider a few typical excuses:

a. "I don't have enough money to set up a budget."

- This is one of the most common reasons given. Don't think that you are exempt from needing to budget your money because you have a limited income. Of all people, you don't have a penny to waste!
- It is imperative that your money is managed properly, allowing it to go farther.

b. "I can control my money without a written budget."

- Oh, really? If you do not have a budget, you are not as in control of your spending as you think you are. Look at your spending. You will be amazed at how much money you waste.

c. "I don't know how to set up a budget."

- Read the rest of this chapter, and you will know exactly what to do. It is time to learn, practice, and succeed.

d. "It's too hard."

- It is harder to get out of debt!

e. "I don't see the need."

- It is difficult to see with your eyes closed. Unfortunately, some people are oblivious to reality and live in a fantasy world. Everybody needs a budget.

f. "I'm doing fine without a budget."

- You would do much better with one. Money that is managed goes much farther.

Notes

- If you have put off setting up a budget, now is the time to tackle it. No more excuses! So, let's get down to business and discuss some simple ideas about establishing a budget.

3. What a Budget Is

- A budget consists of making a written plan to use your money. Budgets include income and expenditure.
- Common sense teaches that you cannot spend more than you earn. However, people frequently overspend because they have no plan on how they will spend their money. If they feel something is a present need, they buy it, regardless if they can afford it or not.
- An out-of-control lifestyle leads to debt and frustration. The average person lives well at the beginning of his pay period and scrounges for money by the end of it. Then, when payday arrives, he celebrates by overspending again.
- Those who keep a budget consider how much money they have and decide how to spend it.
- Even those with a limited income can live comfortably from paycheck to paycheck if they learn to manage their spending.

4. How to Set Up a Budget

- Now that we have seen the importance of a budget, let's discuss how to set one up.
- If you have never made a budget before, you will need some guidance.
- So, consider seven steps for making a monthly budget:

a. Step 1: Make a list of all the things for which you need money and put them into categories.

- What do you need money for? I'm sure that several things come to mind. For example, you need money for giving, eating, driving, housing, etc. Each person's list may differ slightly, but a few general expenses apply to most. Here is a suggested list of budget categories along with sample subcategories:

1) ***Giving*** – Include your tithe, offering, and ministry expenses.
2) ***Home*** – Include your rent/mortgage payment, electricity, phone, water, repairs, cleaning items, and appliance

NOTES

replacement. Keep in mind that many lenders suggest that a maximum of 25-30 percent of your monthly income should be spent on a mortgage.

3) ***Automobile*** – Include money for payments, fuel, insurance, repairs, and licensing.
4) ***Food*** – Include grocery items and dining out.
5) ***Personal Care*** – Include toiletries, clothing, and haircuts.
6) ***Insurance*** – Include health and life insurance.
7) ***Health*** – Include doctor bills, prescriptions, dental, eyes, and vitamins.
8) ***Savings*** – Include money for savings account, retirement plan, and investment plan.
9) ***Entertainment*** – Include vacation, getaways, and family night expenses.
10) ***School*** – Include tuition, fees, books, supplies, and music lessons.
11) ***Gifts*** – Include money for birthdays, Christmas, anniversary, Valentine's Day, etc.
12) ***Emergency*** – Although some might include this in the *Savings* category, a separate emergency fund makes it easier to distinguish how much money you have available for an emergency.
13) ***Miscellaneous*** – Both husband and wife should have a small amount of cash to use at their discretion. Inevitably, expenses arise that are not in one of the above categories.
14) ***Debt*** – Include all overdue bills and credit card debt. You should only need this envelope if you are just starting your budget. Once you learn a proper budget, you should not be going into debt. When contributing money to this envelope, you will have to make it a higher priority than any luxury items in your budget. For example, if you owe thousands in credit card debt, you have no right to buy a brand-new car or plan a fancy family vacation. Pay your debts, and then you can save for the car or vacation. After paying off your debts, you will have extra cash to use as you please!

NOTES

b. **Step 2: Determine how much money you have, not how much you wish you had.**

- Before you can begin to set money aside for each category, you must first understand you do not have an endless supply of cash.
- If you were to assign a dollar amount to each category based on what you thought you needed, you would find that the total amount needed would far exceed your actual monthly income. Therefore, you have to start with the actual amount of money you earn each month and spend only that amount of money.
- Determine to live within your means.

c. **Step 3: Prioritize your financial obligations.**

- When setting up a budget, you actually choose what you will spend money on.
- Though you cannot choose how much money you earn, you can decide how to use it. As we learned earlier, God must come first. Therefore, the tithe and offering must be deducted from your gross pay.
- Whatever you have remaining can be divided into the other budget categories. If you choose to spend a lot of money on a nice car, you will have less to spend on your housing, food, vacation, etc. Likewise, it would be unwise to spend 50 percent of your income on rent or a mortgage because you would not have enough money to pay for your other monthly expenses. So when looking at a place to live, you have to determine if you can pay all of your other bills if you decide to move there. Resist saying, "I want this and will figure out how to pay for it later."
- Remember, this is your budget, not your friend's. Oftentimes people feel like they have to keep up with the lifestyles of their peers. That is nothing but pride. You do not have to have the same type of car, house, or wardrobe as anyone else. Further, if a friend suggests going on vacation together and you don't have the money for it, don't feel embarrassed. Simply say, "It is not in my budget right now." Spending money you don't have in order to impress people is foolish.

NOTES

d. **<u>Step 4</u>: Assign dollar amounts that you will spend for each category.**

- Remember that some expenses are not paid monthly. For example, most people pay car insurance every six months and licensing annually. You will have to determine the cost and divide it by the number of months you will need to save to pay for it. If licensing costs $300 each year, you will need to set aside $25 each month to ensure you have enough money to pay for it. Failing to budget for it would mean that you will have a $300 bill that you are not prepared to pay; and if you put it on your credit card, you will have a debt that will begin to grow because of interest charges.
- Because you cannot spend more money than you have available, be sure to add up the amounts from each category to ensure they do not exceed your monthly income. If the total is higher than what you earn, you will have to go back and lower amounts in some of the categories. It may take a few attempts to rearrange how you want to spend your money; but when you finish, you will be excited about having a plan that will work.
- If you realize that you absolutely do not have enough money to meet your expenses, you may have to consider finding a new job or changing careers. Although working a second job or extended hours may be necessary for a short time, beware that you do not allow thirst for money to hinder your walk with the Lord or your duties at home.
- It is far better to forgo some of the niceties of life than to hurt your family. Solomon cautioned, "Better *is* a dinner of herbs where love is, than a stalled ox and hatred therewith" (Proverbs 15:17).

e. **<u>Step 5</u>: Make an envelope for each budget item.**

- After deciding how much money you want to place in each category of your budget, make an envelope for each subcategory. For instance, let's consider the automobile category. If you decide that you will spend $200 a month toward purchasing a car, $150 on fuel, $100 on insurance, $75 on repairs, and $25 on licensing, then you would place those amounts in separate envelopes. Having one envelope labeled "Automobile" would make

NOTES

it difficult to keep track of all the individual expenses for your car. Instead of spending $150 per month on fuel, you might take $200 a month because you see the cash in the envelope. However, when it comes time to pay the licensing fees, you won't have any money because you spent it on fuel.

- Once you fill all of your envelopes, you are ready to put your financial plan into practice. (3 ½" x 6 ½" – No. 7 Brown Coin Envelopes are the perfect size and are available at most office supply stores.)

f. **Step 6: Be faithful to your envelopes.**

- Only take money from an envelope to pay for expenses related to that category. Once you run out of cash, stop spending money on things in that category until you get paid again. When you start to run low on cash, you will naturally begin to be more careful with the remaining amounts.
- It is tempting to look at envelopes that seem to have a lot of money in them and want to use some of it for other expenses. However, a decision to spend that budgeted money will leave you short when bills come in later. For example, your car has been running well for months and your repair envelope has $1,000 in it. Because you do not foresee any immediate problems with your car, you decide to use the money on a new computer. What will you do two weeks later when your transmission goes out? You will go into debt! Again, I stress, do not spend money you do not have budgeted.
- Once you begin controlling your money, you will find that your spending habits will greatly change. In fact, you may even cut back so much on spending that you will begin to build a surplus in some of your envelopes. For instance, let's say you decided to plan your trips to the store better and went shopping once a week instead of four times a week. Over the course of a month, you will have taken twelve fewer trips to the store. Not only did you save yourself a lot of time, you also spent a lot less on fuel. If each trip to the store cost $4 in fuel, you will have saved $48 over the month. Doing that for two months gives you almost $100 extra in your envelope. In

NOTES

this case, you can use some of this money for something special.

- What about emergencies? Certainly, unexpected expenses will arise, and that is why you should contribute to an emergency envelope on a monthly basis. Many experts believe that your emergency savings should be equal to three months of your current salary, enabling you to endure a financial crisis, such as losing your job. No matter what, do not touch emergency money unless you have an actual emergency, or you will be sorry when a real problem arises.

g. **Step 7: Trust God to meet your needs.**

- You can expect the Lord to provide for you when you have followed His guidelines for money management. However, just because you have a budget does not mean that God will not test your faith.
- Because the Lord wants us to trust Him for our daily bread, He will allow our budget to be disturbed at times in order to keep us depending upon Him. He never wants us to think our wisdom and planning are sufficient. So, when you follow God and things seem to go wrong, look to Him to get you through your trial.

CONCLUDING THOUGHTS:

✓ It makes no sense to spend forty hours a week making money and little to no time planning how to spend it. Common sense tells us that we ought to get serious about budgeting what we have worked so hard to get.

✓ Developing a budget is not easy if you have never done it before. There will be some trial and error as you try to manage your money, but do not think your efforts are in vain. The fact that you are making an attempt to straighten things out will bring great improvements to your financial situation.

✓ Additionally, it is a good idea to get some godly advice on setting up a budget. Your pastor should be able to help you get started. Then, once you begin, be sure to have someone review your budget with you from time to time to ensure you are on the right track.

✓ Keeping a budget brings great peace of mind to your financial outlook because you are confident about meeting your family's needs. It also brings great joy when you learn to save money in

NOTES

your envelopes and are able to purchase things with cash that you once bought on credit. Can you imagine buying a car with cash instead of getting a loan? It is not only possible but also done by many who have learned to budget properly.

Review Questions

1. What is a steward? a manager
2. List three Biblical principles that suggest we should have a budget. management, organization, counting the cost
3. What excuses have you given for not having or keeping a budget? answers will vary
4. What is a budget? It is a written plan for using money, including income and expenditures.
5. Explain the first step in setting up a budget. Make a list of all expenses and organize them into categories.

Notes

Chapter Eight

Deal with Your Debt

Key Verse: *"The rich ruleth over the poor, and the borrower is servant to the lender"* (Proverbs 22:7).

Introductory Thoughts:

- What do you think when you hear the word *debt*? Do thoughts of peace and happiness come to mind?
- In most cases, guilt and regret flood the hearts of those who have the dark cloud of debt hanging over them. Let's face it, receiving a bill in the mail never brings the same amount of joy that getting a check does.
- If you are in debt or contemplating going in debt, this chapter is for you.
- Many reasons contribute to accumulating debt. As we will see, debt becomes a problem when you are unable to pay it.
- The majority of our money woes come from mismanagement, covetousness, overspending, poor planning, or carelessness.
- Although we are usually to blame for most of our debt problems, some circumstances are beyond our control. For instance, we cannot always prevent an unexpected emergency or major health problem that puts us thousands of dollars in debt.
- Despite your circumstances, you are responsible to pay your debts.
- Before going any further in our discussion of debt, let's determine if debt is always sinful.

1. The Debate Over Debt

- Some believe it is sin to have any kind of debt, while others believe that debt is only wrong if it is not paid.
- Certainly when a leading financial consultant such as Dave Ramsey says, "I am duty bound to tell you: *Dump Debt*. That's right—do not borrow money," he must have some good reasons.[8]

Notes

NOTES

- So, how do we know if borrowing money is sinful, foolish, or acceptable? Let's examine the Scriptures.

a. Understand the Terms

- It is easy to get confused about debt if you do not consider the words and concepts involved. Let's consider a few terms:

1) *Lend*
   - The word *lend* is defined, "To grant to another for temporary use, on the express or implied condition that the thing shall be returned."[9]
   - God does not forbid people from lending. In fact, it is often commended in the Bible. "A good man sheweth favour, and lendeth: he will guide his affairs with discretion" (Psalm 112:5).
   - That does not mean that all people who lend are good but that good people are willing to help those who have legitimate needs.
   - Further, the Lord even instructed the Israelites to lend to the poor who were in great need. "If there be among you a poor man of one of thy brethren . . . thou shalt open thine hand wide unto him, and shalt surely lend him sufficient for his need" (Deuteronomy 15:7-8).
   - In regards to our enemies, Jesus tells us to "lend, hoping for nothing again" (Luke 6:35). So, at times, lending is actually encouraged.
2) *Borrow*
   - This word means, "To take from another by request and consent, with a view to use the thing taken for a time, and return it."[10]
   - Borrowing starts at an early age. Children borrow books from the library, toys from their friends, and paper from their classmates.
   - If lending is permissible, borrowing must also be allowed. The practice of borrowing is not necessarily evil, nor is it strictly condemned in the Bible. However, this does not mean that all forms of borrowing are acceptable.

- Larry Burkett aptly said, "The Bible does not teach that you can never borrow; it teaches that borrowing is hazardous if done unwisely."[11]

3) *Credit*
   - *Credit* is defined as a "transfer of goods in confidence of future payment."[12]
   - Credit allows both lender and borrower to complete a transaction.
   - Because lending and borrowing are permitted in the Scripture, credit must also be acceptable in certain situations.
   - While it is true that credit can create enormous problems, the notion that all credit is bad is unfounded. Burkett stated that "the misuse of credit—not credit itself—is the problem."[13] However, just because credit is available does not mean we should avail ourselves to it so readily.
   - The Scriptures imply that borrowing was permitted to supply genuine needs, not to cater to covetousness. Though the Lord allows borrowing, He certainly does not approve of most of it going on today!
4) *Debt*
   - *Debt* means, "That which is due from one person to another, whether money, goods, or services; that which one person is bound to pay or perform to another . . . . It is a common misfortune or vice to be in debt."[14]
   - It is interesting how the definitions of lend, borrow, and credit carry no negative connotation. However, once we get to the word *debt*, that all changes.
   - Even the definition hints at possible misfortune or vice. When credit is offered too freely, borrowers can quickly take too much and struggle to pay it back.
   - In the Bible, the word *debt* is also defined as sin, trespass, guilt, or crime. That may lend to our aversion to debt. The model prayer urges us to pray, "forgive us our debts" (Matthew 6:12). A parallel passage reads, "forgive us our sins" (Luke 11:4). Because the word sometimes means sin, people often wrongly equate every reference to debt as being evil.

NOTES

NOTES

- What makes a debt wrong is not an agreement to borrow but a failure to repay. "The wicked borroweth, and payeth not again" (Psalm 37:21).
- If a man borrows money from the bank to purchase a house, he makes an agreement to pay a certain amount on a monthly basis. If he and the bank agree with the terms and the man makes his payments as promised, he is not guilty of a trespass against the bank. However, if the man fails to pay his debt to the bank, he is wrong and will suffer consequences. Owing money is not a problem. What is a problem is when a person is either unwilling or unable to repay what he borrows.
- People get in trouble financially because they look at debt as the norm instead of as something to shun. Every Christian should strive to borrow as little as possible for as short a period of time as possible. Truly, the goal of every person should be to be debt free. Mary Hunt, founder of Debt-Proof Living, sums up the subject of debt quite well, "Debt is not ideal . . . . [It] is something tolerated in certain situations and only for defined periods of time under rigid guidelines."[15] Do you get the idea? Debt is not something to seek!

b. What Did the Preacher Say?

- Would a true man of God tell someone to sin?
- If all borrowing was wrong, we would not expect a prophet to tell someone to do it.
- In the Scripture, we have an account of an Old Testament prophet who instructed a widow to borrow from others. When the creditor came to take away her sons, Elisha said, "Go, borrow thee vessels abroad of all thy neighbours, *even* empty vessels; borrow not a few" (2 Kings 4:3). Not only was she told to borrow from others, she was commanded to borrow a great quantity. Moreover, God blessed her for her actions. Therefore, it is irresponsible to make statements that condemn all forms of borrowing.
- If we take "Owe no man any thing" at face value (Romans 13:8), we would have to conclude that both Elisha and the widow were wrong. Furthermore, we

would have to say it is sin for women to borrow a cup of sugar from a neighbor or for a man to use his neighbor's ladder.

- Borrowing is not necessarily sin. In Luke 11:3, Jesus used the phrase, "Friend, lend me..." in one of His parables to teach about prayer. If borrowing was sinful, the Lord would have refrained from using it as an illustration.
- While I am not lobbying for people to go into debt, I am not convinced that the Bible prohibits all manner of debt. Borrowing is not necessarily evil, but it becomes so when you fail to pay it back.

c. What About "Owe no man any thing"?

- Let's consider a passage of Scripture that is often quoted when dealing with the topic of debt. "Render therefore to all their dues: tribute to whom tribute *is due*; custom to whom custom; fear to whom fear; honour to whom honour. Owe no man any thing, but to love one another: for he that loveth another hath fulfilled the law" (Romans 13:7-8). The phrase, *Owe no man any thing,* is a golden nugget to those who condemn every form of debt. The verse seems to imply that you should never borrow anything from anybody for any reason. However, it is always wise to consider the context of a passage to be sure you have a correct understanding of the Scripture. Notice that we are to *Render . . . to all their dues.* What does that mean? It simply means that if you owe something, you should pay it. It was not a command to abstain from borrowing but rather a command to pay what is due to others.
- In this case, Paul told the Roman believers to pay their taxes. A tax was not something that they had borrowed; it was simply a payment they were required to make. So, the command was to pay what was owed, not to abstain from borrowing. When we get to the phrase *Owe no man any thing,* we understand that it simply means to pay what you owe. It does not mention borrowing. We must be careful not to make the Bible say something that it does not expressly say. The context of the passage does not condemn borrowing but warns against not paying.

NOTES

- What practical lesson from this passage can we apply to the matter of debt? Debt is not necessarily wrong unless you fail to pay what is due at the time it is due. However, not all debt is wise just because you can pay it off. There are many instances in which debt is wrong.

NOTES

d. When Is It Wrong to Borrow?

- Just because the Scriptures do not condemn all forms of borrowing, we should not take it as a license to go into debt. The debt crisis in our nation is not a result of borrowing a meager amount for an urgent need like the Bible permits. We should never take the aforementioned passages of Scripture to justify the kind of irresponsible, covetous borrowing practices prevalent today.
- Financing homes and cars that are too extravagant and expensive are two of the biggest causes of debt. Others rack up huge credit card bills simply because they have the "gotta-have-it" syndrome. So, how do we know when it is wrong to borrow? It is usually a bad idea to borrow money when:

1) ***You can't pay it back on time.*** Before borrowing money, you must determine if you will be able to pay it back consistently and quickly. If you know you will struggle to make payments, don't borrow.
2) ***It causes you to break your budget.*** If taking on a new debt causes you to be unable to meet your other financial obligations, it is foolish. If you really need something, cut another item out of your budget to pay for it.
3) ***The interest rate is high.*** You end up paying much more for an item when the interest rate is high. It is better to save up and pay cash for what you want to buy.
4) ***You are buying something because of covetousness.*** Any time you are not content with what God has given to you, it is wrong. Fulfilling the lusts of the flesh is never advisable.
5) ***The value of the item that you purchase depreciates in value faster than you can pay it back.*** For example, a new car loses its value quickly—as soon as you drive it off the lot, you will owe more than the car is worth. That makes financing a new car a bad idea. Financing a home is not usually bad because the value of homes typically

increase over time. Borrowing money to purchase something which gains in value is obviously a better scenario.

6) ***You borrow money for a long period of time.*** The difference in what you pay for a home could be tens of thousands of dollars based on one factor—the length of the mortgage. A fifteen-year loan could cut an amazing amount of interest out of your payments compared to a thirty-year loan.
7) ***You are impatient and cannot wait for God to provide for your needs.*** If you are praying for God to meet a particular need, wait for the answer. Don't try to answer the prayer by going into debt to provide for yourself what you asked God to give you. Rushing ahead of God by grabbing what you want when He does not want you to have it displays a lack of faith. Always remember that God's timing is best.
8) ***Your debt leads to more debt.*** If a new payment causes a shortage to meet other needs, you will have to borrow more money. For instance, getting a payday loan may give you the cash you need today; but it leaves you shorthanded for the next week's expenses. Inevitably, you will need to borrow again. When that happens, you will never get out of the borrowing cycle and will be in bondage. Any debt that causes you to accumulate more debt in the future is wrong!

- In reality, most borrowing fits one of the categories listed above. Therefore, borrowing money is usually the wrong thing to do. If you are trying to justify going into debt, I hope you will reconsider. Rather than looking for excuses to go into debt, we ought to require convincing reasons for doing it. Financing furniture, electronic equipment, clothing, and other nonessential items is certainly not wise.

2. The Consequences of Debt

- Now that we have clarified what kind of debt is wrong, let us now consider what happens when debt becomes unmanageable.

NOTES

- Most companies are not in the business of losing money. Therefore, they expect you to pay and will eventually become aggressive in their efforts to collect their money.
- Regardless of how you incurred your debt, you must realize that failure to pay it will bring undesirable consequences. Let's consider what debt can lead to.

a. Debt Brings Bondage

- Illustration – Dave Olson recalls, "In 1998, I paid just over $1,000 for a new laptop computer, charging it to a credit card. That was a lot of money back then! It was one of those "I-need-to-have-it" purchases. Isn't it amazing how we justify buying things we really want? I knew that I would not have the money to pay off the credit card bill when it arrived, but I figured that I would just pay a little bit at a time. However, that became difficult because I did not even have a budget. Over the next several months, I was unable to pay off the computer, and the interest began to multiply. Because my spending continued to be out of control, my debt grew. I was finding out the hard way that the "buy-now-and-pay-later" philosophy brings bondage. Later that year, I was forced to change my ways. Having accepted the call to a little country church, my salary went down to $300 per week. With our third child on the way, we had to stop the downward spiral before our debt became unmanageable. By developing a tight budget and using the envelope system to manage our cash, we were able to get out of debt in less than a year. If we could do it on a limited income, so can you. What a relief it was to have the burden of debt lifted and escape financial bondage!"
- Bondage involves servitude. Solomon wrote, "The rich ruleth over the poor, and the borrower *is* servant to the lender" (Proverbs 22:7). Every time you overextend yourself financially, you make a pledge to yet another master. As the number of creditors increases, so do the number of demands for payment. Although many people who overspend believe they are exercising financial liberty, they are actually creating heavy burdens with each new debt.
- When collection agencies and bill collectors start calling, it puts tremendous pressure and strain on your life. Some

NOTES

people carry a heavy burden of debt for years and cripple their entire future. To cope with the stress, people find an outlet for the pressure, hoping to escape reality. Some try to entertain their misery away, while others turn to drugs or alcohol. The money spent trying to make themselves feel better just creates more debt. Others hope that they will strike it rich by gambling away what money they do have. However, instead of solving their problems, they only create more trouble.

- Before borrowing money, ask yourself if it is worth becoming a servant to the lender. The more creditors you have, the less control you have over your life and future plans. The bondage of debt shatters the dreams of millions who become enslaved to payment plans instead of empowered by financial freedom.

NOTES

b. Debt Can Damage Your Reputation

- Those who fail to pay their debts develop bad credit and prevent themselves from being able to finance a home or car for many years.
- Even friends will stop assisting you if you cannot be trusted to pay them back. God puts a premium on maintaining an outstanding testimony.
- "A *good* name *is* rather to be chosen than great riches, *and* loving favour rather than silver and gold" (Proverbs 22:1). Because your reputation is more valuable than money, you must work hard at reducing your debt. Not only should you be concerned with how your fellow man sees you, you should consider what God thinks of your debt.
- The Scriptures clearly teach that those who borrow without repaying their debts are wicked—"The wicked borroweth, and payeth not again" (Psalm 37:21).
- The Lord is not happy if you are slack in paying your bills, and life will not go smoothly for you when you fail to please Him.

c. Debt Can Bring Loss

- In most cases, unpaid debt grows because of interest that is added on top of the principle.
- The longer you take to pay it, the more interest you pay; and that leaves even less money for your needs.

- In Elisha's day, debt collectors were so ruthless that they would take children away from their parents to be sold as slaves. The widow who went to Elisha said, ". . . my husband is dead . . . and the creditor is come to take unto him my two sons to be bondmen" (2 Kings 4:1). In some cases, those who failed to pay their bills went to jail.
- Jesus told of a man who was cast "into prison, till he should pay the debt" (Matthew 18:30). Although you might not suffer such drastic results, you may still suffer great loss.
- If you fail to pay your car loan, you will lose your car. Those who do not make their mortgage payments will eventually be homeless. Are you starting to see how terrible unpaid debt can become?

d. Debt Produces Stress

- When debt levels go up, so do stress levels. Because of the tremendous pressure that debt brings, people become frustrated, thinking that there is no way out of their problem. They find themselves being short-tempered with those they love, which often involves friction in marriages. In fact, one of the leading causes of divorce is money problems.
- Strife is looming when one spouse has a problem with covetousness, and the trouble is compounded when both are grabbing for things they cannot afford. Tempers flare when one spends money on something the other deems unnecessary. Then, couples begin to blame one another for their financial woes. "If you hadn't bought that stupid pair of shoes," snaps the husband, which provokes the wife to respond, "Like you really needed that new set of tools! You get mad at me for spending fifty bucks, but it's fine for you to spend two hundred!" What a mess overspending creates!
- Because of covetousness, many couples have needlessly "pierced themselves through with many sorrows" (1 Timothy 6:10). It is sad that marriages are destroyed because couples never learn to deal with their sins of covetousness and poor stewardship. Determine to eliminate debt before it destroys important relationships.

NOTES

e. Debt Leads to Discouragement

- Not only does debt lead to stress and irrational behavior, it also results in discouragement. Those who fail to make a plan to pay off their debt tend to tread water or sink further into the financial abyss. When Luke travelled to Rome with Paul, they faced a raging sea that threatened their lives. After the ordeal he wrote, ". . . all hope that we should be saved was then taken away" (Acts 27:20). It is human nature to not be able to see through the storm clouds; and when a financial tempest beats upon us, it is difficult to remain hopeful.
- It is typical for people who have debt problems to get depressed. Instead of turning to God and seeking a Biblical solution, many have a pity party. Perhaps you have said to yourself, "I'm tired of paying bills and never having any money to enjoy for myself." In reality, you already enjoyed your money before you earned it. That's why you are in debt. What happens when people get discouraged? They look for ways to make themselves happy. Let's face it; spending money makes many people happy. However, when you go and buy something to make yourself feel better, your happiness will turn to sorrow as soon as you get the bill. You can never spend your way out of depression!

f. Debt Can Create Problems When You Die

- It is bad enough to burden yourself with debt, but it is even worse to leave a huge amount of debt for your wife. Nobody plans to die prematurely, but it happens every day. When a husband is fiscally irresponsible, he runs the risk of leaving a mess for his wife to face. How loving and thoughtful is that?
- Every Christian husband should strive to stay current with his bills and make a plan for his departure from this world. A substantial life insurance policy and a detailed will can provide peace of mind to your wife; but if you leave her a mound of debt, the money from the life insurance policy can be eaten up quickly. Failing to pay your debts is wicked. How do you want to be remembered by your wife and children? "The memory of the just *is* blessed: but the name of the wicked shall rot" (Proverbs 10:7). Get out of debt!

NOTES

g. Debt Can Hinder Your Service to God

- Jesus warned, "No man can serve two masters: for either he will hate the one, and love the other; or else he will hold to the one, and despise the other. Ye cannot serve God and mammon" (Matthew 6:24). As we mentioned earlier, the word *mammon* refers to money.
- It is impossible to serve God and money at the same; and when you have accumulated a great deal of debt, you are forced to concentrate much of your time on making money to pay it off, leaving less time for God.

NOTES

3. The Solution to Debt

- How can one get out of debt? Three steps are very important: stop overspending, make a plan to pay your debt, and make hard choices. Let's briefly look at each idea.

a. Stop Spending More Money Than You Earn

- A study revealed that 43 percent of American households spend more money than they make.[16] That means four out of ten reading this book may be in such a predicament. What is the solution? Spend less!
- When you overspend, you have to "underspend" for a while. This means you will have to sacrifice items of luxury, and this will not be easy if you tend to buy everything you want.
- You must learn to tell yourself "No." You may have to give up your smart phone, stop eating out, sell your car and buy a cheaper one, and forget trips to the mall. Your lifestyle has to change, or you will never get out of debt! Got it? Drastically cut spending!
- Once you stop overspending, you will have money to start paying toward your debt. If you continue to build debt, it will seem almost impossible to recover from it.

b. Make a Plan to Pay Off Your Debt

- After you get your spending under control, you will be amazed at how much extra money you will have to pay your debts. Start by making a list of all your creditors and determine how much you will send to each one on a monthly basis. Keep in mind that you need to pay at least the minimum monthly payment indicated on each bill. You can often negotiate a reasonable payment by contacting your creditors. Most companies will be more patient with you if you communicate with them. You can save money in the long run by paying more to the companies who charge higher interest.

- Many financial consultants suggest arranging your debts from smallest to largest. Then, determine how much you can pay toward each bill on a monthly basis, and be faithful to pay down each debt. Soon your first creditor will be paid off. Once that happens, you will be encouraged to continue. Victory is contagious! For every debt that you pay off, you will have more money available to put toward the next debt on the list. Before long, another small debt will be paid in full. Eventually, you will be able to pay off all of your debts. Dave Ramsey calls this process the "Debt Snowball."[17] Other financial advisors have similar plans known by different names.
- Consider a simple example of paying down your debt. Let's say you owe $10,775. After you've set up your budget and stopped wasting money, you noticed that you had an additional $250 each month available to use to pay your debt. As mentioned earlier, you would list your debts from smallest to largest as indicated below.

Debt	Amount Owed	Monthly Payment
Doctor	$120	$30
Dentist	$280	$50
Furniture Store	$775	$50
Credit Card 1	$2,800	$50
Credit Card 2	$6,800	$70

- Now you can assign a dollar amount to pay toward each bill. Obviously, some of your bills will continue to grow due to the interest that will be charged, but don't let that discourage you. Notice that in four months, the doctor bill will be paid off. That gives you an extra $30 per month to put toward the next bill on the list—the dentist bill. Because you have been paying $50 a month to the dentist for four months already, you only owe $80. That means the $30 plus the already budgeted amount of $50 will give you the $80 you need to pay that bill. So, in five months, you will have paid off the first two bills on

Notes

your list! Now you have some momentum. By month six, you only owe $525 to the furniture store (plus whatever interest was charged over those few months); but because you have an extra $80 available (money that you no longer need to pay the doctor and dentist), you will be able to pay $130 per month toward your furniture debt. In just over four more months, debt number three is eliminated. That gives you an extra $130 to put toward Credit Card 1, meaning that you can now pay $180 per month on that debt. Depending on the interest rate, Credit Card 1 will be paid off in full in a couple of years. Then, you put that monthly payment of $180 together with the $70 that you are already paying toward Credit Card 2. Before you know it, you will be debt free!

- In just a few years, you can dissolve over $10,000 in debt just by making a plan and sticking to it. Rather than going further into debt, you can get out of it! Now, imagine saving $250 per month instead of paying debt and interest. In three and a half years, you would have over $10,000 to use as you please! That would give you a better feeling than being $10,000 in debt.
- What enables people to have financial victories like this? The key is to make a budget and follow it. As you eliminate needless spending, you will have money to pay off your debts and save for things that are really important to you.

c. Make Hard Choices

- Let's get back to the widow who had financial problems in Elisha's day. After the woman sought the Lord's help, He provided for her immediate needs. However, He also required her to make some sacrifices. She was expected to take her surplus and pay her bills. The prophet told her, "**Go**, **sell** the oil, and **pay** thy debt, and live thou and thy children of the rest" (2 Kings 4:7, emphasis added). She was supposed to sell what she had and pay her debts. Then, she was to live off the rest. Very few people ever want to part with what they have to pay their debts. Have you ever thought of selling some of your possessions to relieve your indebtedness? That's exactly what God told the widow to do—*Go, sell . . . and pay thy debt.*

NOTES

- Many times the answer to our problems is right in front of us! Selling your dream car and purchasing a more affordable one might be in order if you are struggling to pay your bills. You may say, "That's not fair. I deserve to have my things." Actually, it's not fair for you to have those things at someone else's expense. You are required to pay your bills.
- Too many hold onto their money and buy things they want for themselves instead of paying off their debts, but God warns against such an attitude. "Withhold not good from them to whom it is due, when it is in the power of thine hand to do *it*. Say not unto thy neighbour, Go, and come again, and to morrow I will give; when thou hast it by thee" (Proverbs 3:27-28).
- It is not right to keep money for selfish purposes when you owe it to others. It is sin! For instance, a person who gets a refund from their tax return should never blow it on a vacation until they first pay their outstanding credit card balance, school bill, or high-interest loan. You can enjoy the luxuries of life after you pay back your debt.
- The faster you pay down your debt, the quicker you will have a surplus to use as you see fit. So, get aggressive and be willing to part with things that you can live without. In the end, you will be happy that you did it.

Concluding Thoughts:

✓ Although borrowing money is not always sinful, it can lead to sin.

✓ Beware of going into debt for foolish reasons and always ensure that you are able to repay what you borrow. Those who are not careful will suffer bondage, frustration, and turmoil.

✓ If you are already in debt, make the hard choices that are necessary to get out of it.

✓ Develop a plan and stick to it; but keep in mind that since you did not get into debt overnight, you will not get out of it overnight. Those who apply Biblical solutions and persevere will rejoice in the end.

✓ Finally, if you trust God through this difficult time in your life, it will build your faith and make you more financially stable in the future.

Notes

Review Questions

1. In Proverbs 22:7, what is a borrower called? a servant
2. According to Psalm 112:5, what kind of person lends? a good man
3. What does the phrase, *"Owe no man any thing,"* refer to? It was a command to pay what was due, not a command to refrain from borrowing.
4. Summarize the consequences of debt. bondage, damaged reputation, loss, stress, discouragement, problems at death, hindered service
5. List three solutions to debt. stop spending more than you earn, make a plan to reduce debt, make hard choices

---

[8] Dave Ramsey, *Financial Peace Revisited* (New York: Penguin Putnam, 2003), 70.
[9] Noah Webster, *Noah Webster's 1828 Dictionary of American English* (Franklin: e-Sword, 2000-2014), Digital Library.
[10] Ibid.
[11] Larry Burkett, *Debt-Free Living* (Chicago: Moody Publishers, 2010), 174.
[12] Webster.
[13] Burkett, *Debt-Free Living,* 174.
[14] Webster.
[15] Mary Hunt, *7 Money Rules for Life* (Grand Rapids: Revell, 2012), 124.
[16] Lisa Smith, "Stop Keeping Up With The Joneses—They're Broke Too." *Investopedia,* accessed July 30, 2014, http://www.investopedia.com/articles/pf/07/conspicuous_consumption.asp.
[17] More information about the "Debt Snowball" and other tips about getting out of debt can be found in *The Total Money Makeover* by Dave Ramsey.

Chapter Nine

Beware of Credit Cards

Key Verse: *"The wicked borroweth, and payeth not again"* (Psalm 37:21).

Introductory Thoughts:

- The average credit card debt for American households is over $7,000.[18] That is an alarming statistic, which proves that credit cards make it far too easy to go into debt.
- For most people, using credit cards is a disaster waiting to happen.
- If you are prone to spend money that you do not have, cut up your credit cards immediately! The ability to buy now and pay later leads to debt, especially for those who have demonstrated a weak will in the area of spending. You will never get out of debt using credit cards.
- Discussing credit cards is a sensitive issue with many people.
- People either make excuses for their habit of overspending, or they get offended if you suggest they are not responsible enough to use a credit card. I am not anti-credit card as much as I am against foolish spending.
- People with self-control and good discipline often handle credit cards quite well. As we saw in the previous chapter, credit is not necessarily evil and does not have to lead to unpaid debt.
- Larry Burkett taught, "Credit only turns into debt when we mismanage our finances."[19] Unfortunately, not everyone is a good steward, and that makes credit card use hazardous for the majority of people. Hopefully, you will take a deep breath and objectively consider your use of credit cards.
- After describing how credit cards work, we will consider common problems experienced by credit card holders, an alternative to using credit cards, and tips for those who cannot live without a credit card.

NOTES

1. How Credit Cards Work

- Credit cards allow you to purchase items and services without using cash. Once a month, you are sent a statement which details all of your purchases. To make things easy for you, the credit card company figures a minimum payment that is due that month, allowing you to take your time to pay the balance. However, you will be charged interest on the amount that you do not pay. It is like a small loan with an extremely high interest rate. The longer you take to pay off your balance, the more money you lose. That is how the credit card companies make money.
- Because of the convenience of not having to carry cash, credit cards have gained wide acceptance in our society.

2. Major Problems of Credit Cards

- The road to debt is usually traveled by those with a credit card. Although they are convenient, credit cards pose serious potential problems.

a. Money Can Be Spent Easily

- Let's face it—credit cards make it easy to spend money. Instead of thinking over a purchase and checking to see if you have enough money in your budget, you have instant access to funds to purchase whatever you want.
- Unfortunately, millions of Americans overspend simply because "plastic money" is readily accessible.

b. Debt Can Accumulate Quickly

- A second problem with credit cards is that they allow you to accumulate debt.
- Sixty percent of people who use credit cards do not pay off their balances each month.[20] That means the majority of people who use them are in debt!
- When you pay off your credit card every month, you avoid paying rip-off interest rates. However, once you begin overspending, you will be unable to pay off the balance at the end of each month. The credit card company acts like the hero because they enable you to pay all of your other bills and provide a nice low monthly payment. Over time, the monthly payment increases because your debt increases. Then, like millions of Americans, you will owe thousands in credit card debt

Notes

and become crippled financially for years until you figure out a way to pay off your debt.

- Sadly, unnecessary clouds of grief and frustration hover over too many households due to the irresponsible use of credit cards.

c. Easy Credit Often Feeds Covetousness

- Credit cards enable weak-willed people to yield to the temptation of covetousness.
- Spending is an addiction to many, and credit cards allow them to "get their fix." If you are addicted to spending, having a credit card makes it easier for you to indulge in instant gratification.
- Paul reminds us, ". . . make not provision for the flesh, to *fulfil* the lusts *thereof*" (Romans 13:14). In any area of our lives, we should not make it easier for ourselves to sin. So, if you cannot control your spending, do not have a credit card.
- George Bowman, author and financial consultant, wisely said, "Wants always exceed income, and the gap cannot be filled by use of consumer credit."[21]
- We must never use credit to commit the sin of covetousness.

3. Great Offers

- The credit card industry is big business. They make a fortune off the interest that they charge people. Because the credit card business is so competitive, companies offer great reward programs. If you spend enough money, you can get plane tickets, gift cards, hotel stays, and meals at fine restaurants with the rewards you earn. Most cards give at least one point per dollar spent along with opportunities to earn bonus points. People who are successful at managing their money often end up with free stuff by using credit cards. So, how can credit card companies give away so much merchandise without going out of business?
- Let's use a common credit card offer to illustrate the point. People are approached every day by smiling credit card representatives at airports across the country offering enough points in their program for a free flight just for signing up for the card. The company is willing to give away free flights because they know that most will soon overspend and be

Notes

unable to pay off their monthly balance. Before long, not only will the customer have paid for that flight through interest payments, but he will continue giving the credit card his hard-earned money as long as he carries an unpaid balance. So, how free was the flight? How great was the offer?

- In many cases, people tend to spend more when using a credit card. Consumers justify purchases because they are earning points. Even those who are good at paying off their monthly balance are tempted to spend a little extra on their credit card just to earn a few more points. Do the math. Does it make sense to spend $500 unnecessarily just to earn a free $50 gift card? Believe it or not, it happens.
- For those who are great money managers, reward programs provide nice fringe benefits. However, typical credit card holders lose far more than they gain and foot the bill for the entire rewards program with their interest payments. For most, the benefits simply do not outweigh the risks of having credit cards.

4. A Good Alternative—The Debit Card

- Many argue that they need a credit card for travelling, online purchases, or to earn reward points for free merchandise. However, debit cards can do just about everything a credit card can do for you without charging you interest or enabling you go into debt.

a. How Debit Cards Work

- Debit cards are offered through your local bank and are tied to your bank account.
- VISA and MasterCard are payment processing networks that allow people to make purchases without cash. In the past, they were associated solely with credit card accounts, but now bank accounts can use those networks through debit cards. What makes them great is that they allow you to make the same transactions that credit cards allow you to make. Because they are accepted just like credit cards, you can make everyday purchases with money that you already have in the bank. VISA and MasterCard withdraw the money from your bank account instead of sending the charge to a credit card company. Prior to making purchases, you can take budgeted money

NOTES

from your envelopes and deposit it into your bank account. Doing this ensures that you can spend only the amount of money you have available, preventing you from incurring more debt. So, you have the same conveniences that credit cards provide without having to worry about overspending or paying interest rates.

- When using a debit card, you cannot spend more money than is available in your bank account, but you will still have to be careful not to "rob Peter to pay Paul."
- Consider an example. Let's say you plan on going shopping. You put $50 from your clothing envelope and $150 from your food envelope into your bank account. However, you find some great deals at the mall. So, you spend $100 on clothing instead of $50. That means you will have $50 less to spend on groceries. I hope your family won't mind eating "cardboard" pizza or beans and weenies instead of their usual meals. After that happens a time or two, you will learn to control your spending. If that happened with the credit card, you would have probably bought the clothes and the normal amount of groceries, resulting in $50 debt that you could not pay.

b. "What About My Rewards Points?"

- Let's get back to rewards programs. What if you can't bear giving up your credit card because you like earning rewards points? Well, some banks offer debit cards that give rewards points.
- Earning points without accumulating debt provides the best of both worlds. If your bank does not offer such a debit card, you can always find a new bank that does, or you can forgo the rewards. It's your choice.

c. Online Shopping

- Shopping online makes it convenient to get goods quickly; but, unfortunately, it also makes it easy to spend money.
- Oftentimes, those with spending problems are also big online shoppers.
- If you need to make a purchase using the Internet, make the purchase using your debit card after depositing cash into your account from the appropriate envelope in your budget. Doing this will allow you to ensure that the

NOTES

money is actually available and will prevent you from spending money you do not have.

- Using a credit card would allow you too much freedom to buy without knowing for certain that you have the money to pay for it. Debit cards can help eliminate a lot of impulsive shopping!

d. Travelling with Debit Cards

- Plan the amount of money you will need for the trip by taking the necessary funds from your envelopes and depositing them into your account before you travel. That will ensure you only spend money that you have, preventing you from encountering more debt.
- What if the car breaks down? In most cases, you can transfer funds electronically and have enough money to pay a mechanic by the next day. However, for peace of mind, you can take a small amount of money from your emergency fund and have it in the account just in case you run into a problem on the trip that requires immediate resources.
- Be careful not to waste your emergency money to buy everybody in the family a T-shirt at your favorite tourist attraction.

5. What About Building Credit?

- It is true that credit cards allow you to establish credit with banks, enabling you to get a loan for a home. However, obtaining a small personal loan from your local bank can also build your credit.
- Simply borrow a small amount and set that money aside to pay back the loan each month. Don't touch it for any reason! It is not your money; it belongs to the bank.
- You will also have to budget a small amount of cash to pay the interest on the loan.
- After making the scheduled payments, never being late, you will have proven yourself worthy of more credit.

6. Dealing with Emergencies

- Emergencies will arise, and some of them will cost you a lot of money. This leads to a good question—are credit cards good for emergencies? Yes and no. Let me explain. Those who work their budget properly will have an emergency fund

NOTES

to get them through an unexpected crisis. Because you may not have access to your cash while stranded at an airport in a foreign land, a credit card would be a blessing to have. In most cases your debit card will do you no good unless you have a lot of money sitting in your bank account; but that is rare. Those who are financially responsible can pay an emergency expense with a credit card and pay it off with the money that is available in their emergency fund.

- However, a person who does not have an emergency fund and uses a credit card for his emergency situations is not wise. This individual will go into debt just like the uncontrolled online shopper does. Regardless of how you accumulate it, you will have to pay your debt.

7. What About Foreign Travel?

- Personally, I would not travel overseas without a credit card.
- No amount of advance planning can equip you to handle life-threatening emergencies.
- Many countries can become hostile without a moment's notice, and the fastest way to secure plane tickets is by using a credit card. In some instances, there is no time to wait for a bank transfer, rendering debit cards ineffective. Further, many foreign medical facilities do not accept American health insurance.
- Illustration – Dave Olson explains, "Serving overseas as a missionary, I often found myself paying with a credit card to receive needed medical treatment. In cases of foreign travel, a credit card might save your life."

8. Tips for Controlling a Credit Card

- As you can see, in most cases, it is possible to live without credit cards. In fact, millions of people in other countries do it every day!
- However, if you have proven yourself to be frugal, disciplined, and in control of your spending through successful budgeting, you might be part of a minority of people who can use a credit card responsibly. If so, here are a couple of tips that might help you.

a. Keep Your Credit Limit Low

- Some credit card companies want you to have a high limit so you will spend more money. While that makes

NOTES

them more money, it can enable you to spend far more than you should. Keep your credit limit low to ensure that you will never go too far into debt. For instance, if you never make purchases more than $2,000 during any given month, set your limit accordingly. A low limit is a safeguard against increased debt.

b. Use Your Envelopes

- After every purchase using a credit card, immediately pull the money from the appropriate envelope in your budget and place it in another envelope marked "Credit Card." Failing to do it immediately often means you will forget to do it, causing you to think you have more money available to spend than you actually have.
- When your credit card statement comes in, take the money out of the *Credit Card* envelope and deposit it into the bank before writing a check to pay the bill. Again, I stress, do not charge anything to a credit card if you do not have money in your envelopes to pay for it.
- Even before the era of credit cards, Thomas Jefferson wisely stated, "Never spend your money before you have it."[22]

c. Monitor Your Spending Habits

- Remember that even thrifty people must be aware that spending can quickly get out of control.
- If you find that you are overspending and cannot pay off your monthly balance, it may be time to cancel your credit card. At the very least, stop using the card, saving it for emergencies. Then, begin using your debit card or cash for your purchases.

9. Should I Transfer My Balance?

- Much of what we have discussed has been aimed at making a choice about whether to use credit cards or not. For some, you already have a lot of credit card debt. What should you do?
- For starters, you ought to consider cutting up your credit card so that you do not continue to go further in debt. Then, you might want to transfer your credit card balance to another credit card which offers lower interest rates. Credit card companies will offer little to no interest for several months to

NOTES

new customers. Why do they do that? They know people with big balances have spending problems, and they figure that you will continue spending money and rack up more debt that you cannot pay. At the end of the promotional interest rate, the rate goes up; and you are hit with huge interest fees. However, you don't have to continue to fall to ploys of credit card companies.

- Here are a couple of tips. Be sure that there are no fees for transferring your balance. If you have to pay 3 to 5 percent of your balance in order to receive a lower rate, you may lose more money by transferring.[23] Also, some companies require that you pay the entire balance by the end of the promotional period, and failing to do so may cost you another fee.
- If you decide to transfer a balance, your existing card will be reduced to a zero balance. That might sound good; but if you do not cancel the card, you could be tempted to use it again and go further into debt. Understand that cancelling a bunch of credit cards all at once can adversely affect your credit rating,[24] but so will spending more money on the card if you cannot pay it off. So, if you decide to transfer a balance from a high interest rate card to a lower one, consider cancelling the first account. Next, destroy the card that is tied to the new credit card account. Destroying the card will not relieve you of paying the debt, but it will prevent you from making more unnecessary charges.
- Finally, beware of playing the transfer game. Continually adding new credit cards can be seen by credit rating agencies as a plan to spend more money, which can hurt your credit rating.[25] Instead of seriously working at paying off their balances, some people just shift the debt from one credit card to another for years.
- Don't forget what kind of person refuses to take responsibility for paying his debts—*"The wicked borroweth, and payeth not again"* (Psalm 37:21).
- If you can save money by transferring a balance, do so; but be sure to work hard at paying it off as soon as possible.

NOTES

CONCLUDING THOUGHTS:

NOTES

- ✓ As we have seen, credit cards are convenient, but they can lead to overspending and debt.
- ✓ Debit cards allow you to do almost everything that a credit card can do for you. So, if you struggle with credit cards, consider switching over to a debit card. Many people do quite well using a debit card for their everyday purchases and keep a credit card available for absolute emergencies. That may be a good plan for you, too.
- ✓ If you choose to use a credit card for everyday purchases, monitor your spending carefully, and avoid the temptation to overspend.
- ✓ Remember, if you find yourself using the credit card for "emergencies" such as buying something on sale, you are heading for trouble.

REVIEW QUESTIONS

1. According to Psalm 37:21, what kind of person borrows and does not repay? wicked
2. List three major problems with credit cards. money is spent easily, debt accumulates quickly, covetousness is fed
3. What is a good alternative to a credit card? a debit card
4. What is another way to build credit without using a credit card? Get a small personal loan and repay it.
5. Summarize the three tips for controlling credit cards. keep credit limits low, use envelopes, monitor spending

---

[18] Tim Chen, "American Credit Card Debt Statistics: 2014," *Nerd Wallet*, accessed July 31, 2014, http://www.nerdwallet.com/blog/credit-card-data/average-credit-card-debt-household/.
[19] Larry Burkett, *Money Matters for Teens* (Chicago: Moody Press, 2000), 111.
[20] Dave Ramsey, *The Total Money Makeover* (Nashville: Nelson Books, 2003), 127.
[21] George Bowman, *How to Succeed with Your Money* (Chicago: Moody Press, 1982), 45.
[22] Berger, "Top 100 Money Quotes of All Time."
[23] Miranda Marquit, "Should I Do a Balance Transfer," *Bible Money Matters*, accessed August 1, 2014, http://www.biblemoneymatters.com/should-you-do-a-balance-transfer/.
[24] Hunt, *7 Money Rules for Life*, 172.
[25] Ibid, 124.

Chapter Ten

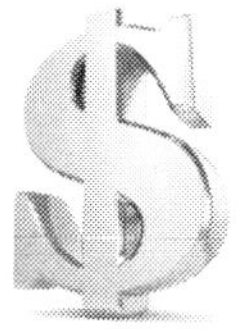

Save Money

<u>Key Verse</u>: *"...strong men retain riches"* (Proverbs 11:16).

<u>Introductory Thoughts</u>:

- Most people agree that it is good to save money, but few make it a priority.
- In this age of instant gratification, many people tend to live for the present moment and think little about the future. Instead of saving money, this covetous generation is obsessed with spending it.
- We must remember that a decision to spend now is a decision to have less for another day.
- If you are the type that lets money flow through your fingers like water, it's time to get serious about saving a portion of your income on a regular basis.

1. The Purpose of Saving

- Obviously, the general concept of saving money is to have more for a later time.
- Most of us have heard of the saying, "A dollar saved is a dollar earned." In reality, when you figure in what you pay in taxes, a dollar you save is worth more than a dollar earned. Further, the more you save, the less you have to earn in the future. People who fail to save have to work harder and longer than those who set some of their earnings aside.
- Previous generations were much more frugal than we are today. Only in recent history has the majority of Americans begun to accept the notion that it is normal to spend more money than they make, leaving nothing for savings. It has not always been so in our nation.
- While it is true that previous generations may not seem to have been as wealthy, what they had belonged to them, not the bank. Today, people live in big houses, drive expensive

Notes

cars, and dress in the latest fashions; but much of what they possess has been bought on credit. In reality, what a person buys on credit is not really his own. It is borrowed until it is paid off.

- Much of the wealth in our society is actually a smoke screen. When hard economic times come, many lose everything because it was never theirs in the first place. What ever happened to spending less than you earn, building savings, and preparing for the future? Since our society has strayed from the Bible, covetousness has increased and thriftiness has decreased.
- The mind-set that emphasizes spending instead of saving has led to the financial ruin of multitudes. Instead of spending as much as possible, we ought to save as much as we can. This is a foreign concept to many in our society but should be a way of life for every Christian. Let's consider a few reasons why we ought to save.

a. Saving Is Wise to Do

- Consider the comparison that God makes between the saver and the spender. "*There is* treasure to be desired and oil in the dwelling of the wise; but a foolish man spendeth it up" (Proverbs 21:20). The one who reserves some of his treasure is called *wise,* but notice what the one who spends all of his money is called—*a foolish man.* Which kind of person are you: one who saves some or one who spends everything he makes? If you squander all you have now, you will be unable to meet other needs that will arise in the future.
- If you would like to double your money, start saving the same amount that you used to overspend. Instead of accumulating debt, you will build savings.
- The person who learns to save enjoys blessings that many only dream of. First, he has no reason to borrow and get in debt. Second, he has money set aside for emergencies when they arise. Third, he has money available to help others in need. Spenders often want to help others but cannot do it unless they go in debt to do so.

NOTES

b. Saving Empowers

- How many times have your plans been foiled because you did not have enough money to do what you wanted to do? Rather than saying, "I always wanted to do that," we ought to make plans to save and make some of our dreams come true. Would you like to own a house instead of rent? or go on a special vacation? It may take a while; but making a plan to save a little each pay period will add up over time, making it possible to reach your goals. However, if you only wish for something without developing a strategy to accomplish it, your dreams will fail to become reality.
- Think about the cost Noah incurred while building the ark. "By faith Noah, being warned of God of things not seen as yet, moved with fear, prepared an ark to the saving of his house" (Hebrews 11:7). This great man of faith worked for decades, preparing to take his family on a once-in-a-lifetime cruise. As he set aside money and materials, he was empowered to do something nobody else had ever done. In this instance, saving allowed Noah to fulfill the will of God for his life. If he had spent all of his money on frivolous purchases, he and his family would have perished with the others. I wonder how many people fail to fulfill God's will because they are financially irresponsible.
- The virtuous woman in Proverbs was empowered to help others. Several verses record her hard work and thriftiness; and because she did not waste her money, she was not only able to provide for her family but relieve the afflicted. "She stretcheth out her hand to the poor; yea, she reacheth forth her hands to the needy" (Proverbs 31:20). Not only was she a blessing to others, she earned eternal rewards for herself.
- Look at the promise made to those who sacrifice for the Lord, "For God *is* not unrighteous to forget your work and labour of love, which ye have shewed toward his name, in that ye have ministered to the saints, and do minister" (Hebrews 6:10). We may conclude that saving money enables us to be a blessing to others and secure favor with God for ourselves.

NOTES

c. Saving Prepares for the Future

- I heard the results of a recent poll which reported that one in four Americans have no money set aside for a "rainy day." In other words, 25 percent of our population is completely unprepared if something goes wrong with either the economy or their personal finances. That is an alarming statistic. Of those who do have savings, many only have a meager amount set aside. Do you have enough to weather a financial storm?
- Having faced a significant recession recently, many economic experts suggest a larger fiscal problem is looming. Just if or when a crash to our economy may occur, nobody knows. However, wise people do not take legitimate warnings about trouble lightly. "A prudent *man* foreseeth the evil, and hideth himself: but the simple pass on, and are punished" (Proverbs 22:3).
- Failing to set money aside in times of prosperity could adversely determine your fate when trouble comes. You may ask, "What if the economy does not suffer?" My answer—Great! You are never worse off because you saved money. Even if the country does not face a huge crisis, you may experience one personally. Certainly, you will never regret being prepared.
- One note of caution should be mentioned about preparing for the future. God does not want us to save out of fear of uncertain times. There is a difference between planning and worrying. Planning is a demonstration of faith, and worrying results from a lack of faith.
- Consider the words that Jesus spoke, "Take therefore no thought for the morrow: for the morrow shall take thought for the things of itself. Sufficient unto the day *is* the evil thereof" (Matthew 6:34). The phrase *Take therefore no thought* refers to being anxious about a matter. Christ does not want us to be worried about things we cannot change. Obviously, based on the other Scriptures we have read, He wants us to plan; but He does not want us to worry.
- So, be full of faith that God will provide for your future, not full of fear of having nothing one day.

NOTES

d. Saving Enables Giving

- We must be careful that our motivation to save is not based upon covetousness.
- In His introduction to the parable about the rich man, Jesus warned against covetousness by saying, "beware of covetousness" (Luke 12:15). In the parable that follows, the rich man had so much substance, he did not know what to do with it all. Deciding to build bigger barns to save even more, he said to himself, "Soul, thou hast much goods laid up for many years; take thine ease, eat, drink, *and* be merry" (Luke 12:19). The man had saved for selfish purposes. He posed this question to himself, "What shall I do, because I have no room where to bestow my fruits?" (Luke 12:17). A better decision than building bigger barns would have been to give some of it to God and others in need.
- Because this man's savings were all for himself, Jesus pronounced him a fool. He was not condemned for being successful but for failing to give some of his savings to the Lord. Christ's application to all of us is, "So *is* he that layeth up treasure for himself, and is not rich toward God" (Luke 12:21). In other words, if our savings are only for ourselves, we are foolish. If God blesses you with riches, be rich toward God! He likes to give to those who will be conduits of His grace.
- In a real sense, your tithe and offering are something that you save in order to give to God. Notice the wording, "Upon the first *day* of the week let every one of you lay by him in store, as *God* hath prospered him, that there be no gatherings when I come" (1 Corinthians 16:2). The phrase *lay by him in store* refers to reserving money for the purpose of giving. Malachi refers to God's house as the *storehouse,* where the Lord's money is saved for use in His work. It is Biblical to save money for God. Sometimes we are tempted to think that after we have tithed we can keep the rest for ourselves. However, at times, the Lord may want part of our savings, too.
- Will we be like the rich man in the parable who wanted to keep it all for himself, or will we be like Mary who sacrificed a box of ointment which was valued at nearly a year's salary? If our savings are off limits to God, our motive for saving should be questioned. Being covetous

NOTES

as the rich man may secure the same title Christ gave to him—*Thou fool.*

NOTES

2. The Power of Saving

- Saving money is a bit like exercise—it is difficult in the beginning but gets easier as time goes on. Once you begin to see your savings grow, excitement will lead you to continue saving. Further, you will begin to guard your money more carefully because of the hard work that it took to build a reserve.
- Those with money tend to have it for a reason—they have developed a habit of saving instead of spending. So, if you will save with as much zeal as you have spent, debt will be replaced by assets.

a. Saving Takes Power

- The ability to save reveals much about a person's character.
- Notice that saving money is a sign of strength. "A gracious woman retaineth honour: and strong *men* retain riches" (Proverbs 11:16). Strong people are able to retain some of their wealth, but weak people spend all of their money. When we look at all of the uncontrolled spending we see in society, we must conclude that our world is filled with weak people. What do your saving habits reveal about you? Are you weak or strong? If you can never hold onto any of your money, perhaps you are not as strong as you thought.
- Thankfully, God promises to give strength to those who want it. "Fear thou not; for I *am* with thee: be not dismayed; for I *am* thy God: I will strengthen thee; yea, I will help thee; yea, I will uphold thee with the right hand of my righteousness" (Isaiah 41:10).
- Your financial problems can completely turn around once you decide to follow God's plan and seek His strength to do so. What a promise! Not only does God want us to save, He desires to give us the strength to do so.

b. Saving Creates Power

- Let me illustrate the power of saving money with a simple story. Two families decide to take a three hundred mile trip through a remote area. Since the road has no fuel stations, the first family equips their vehicle with a reserve tank. The second family knows that their vehicle will have just enough fuel to make it so they don't bother with any reserve fuel. So, they start off on their journey. About two hundred miles into their trip, they discover that a bridge on the main road is out, and they will have to take an alternate route which would add another one hundred miles to their journey. Which family will make it? Obviously, it will be the one with the reserve tank. The other family will be stranded. Can you see the benefit of having reserves?

- In life, those who plan ahead and have money reserved will go farther than those who fail to save. Because life is filled with detours, we must all plan for them financially. Many are stranded along life's road because they failed to have a little cash set aside for unexpected events.
- Let's consider an example from the Bible. While Joseph was imprisoned in Egypt, God gave Pharaoh a dream which troubled him greatly. As we know, Joseph was released from prison to stand before Pharaoh to interpret the dream. The land was to enjoy seven years of plenty followed by seven years of terrible famine. The Lord gave Joseph wisdom to suggest reserving 20 percent of the harvest during the good years to endure the troublesome times that were just around the corner. Not only did he suggest the plan, he executed it; and in the process, he saved a multitude of lives, including his own family. Saving had a powerful effect!
- Through saving cash, you will be able to pay for unexpected car repairs, emergency dentist appointments, and other crises. Saving gives you the power to provide without going in debt.

3. The Plan for Saving

- Now that we have considered the purpose and power of saving money, let's learn some principles that will help us as we develop a plan to save. We will answer a couple of simple questions that people have about saving and investing money.
- When should you begin saving? Immediately! Make a plan to save something out of every paycheck. It may be small to begin with, but it is vital to begin right away. Some wonder

Notes

if it wise to save while they still owe debt. Is it? Yes. Because you must be prepared for unexpected expenses, saving money in an emergency fund will help prevent further debt. So, by all means do not delay.

- Have you ever wondered how much money you should save? Obviously, the more you can save the better off you will be in the future. However, nobody can save 100 percent without robbing from God and foregoing everyday needs. Besides, the Lord wants us to enjoy a portion of what He has provided for us. So, we should not set out to save it all.
- The key to saving is to determine a workable amount based on your current income and your future needs. After getting out of debt and establishing an emergency fund, Dave Ramsey recommends saving 15 percent of your income in retirement plans.[26] Although Joseph suggested to Pharaoh to save 20 percent, those were special circumstances during a time of great plenty. In sluggish economic times, it may not be possible to save 15-20 percent. In reality, God never told us what percentage of our money ought to be saved. However, He did not leave us to try to figure it all out on our own. Wisdom is promised to all who seek it from the Lord. "If any of you lack wisdom, let him ask of God, that giveth to all *men* liberally, and upbraideth not; and it shall be given him" (James 1:5). If you can only save 5 or 10 percent, you are better off than the one who saves nothing. If you do not have a goal, you will probably not save much at all. Saving something is always better than nothing!
- Situations will arise in life that will prevent you from being able to save anything at all for a season, but that does not mean you are backslidden. Just before healing the lame man, Peter said, "Silver and gold have I none" (Acts 3:6). Although Peter did not have any savings on hand, he certainly had God's power. Spirituality is not measured by the size of one's savings account. If you recall, that is the false teaching of the prosperity gospel. Don't mourn because you may not have much to save at the present moment. Do your best to get out of debt and cut your spending; and in due time, you will be able to save more.
- Where should you put the bulk of your money: savings or investments? In the initial stages, it is wise to put more into savings than investments, especially until you have an emergency fund well established. After securing your short-

NOTES

term future by protecting money in savings, you can begin contributing more to investment opportunities.

- People have saved money in a variety of ways over the years. I have heard of people who have buried it, hidden it in the walls of their home, stuffed furniture with it, and put it in old shoe boxes. Let's consider the most common options for saving your money.

a. Cash

- During the Great Depression, thousands of banks failed and people lost all the money that they had deposited. For decades thereafter, many were skeptical about using banks to protect their hard-earned money. To ensure that such a catastrophe would never happen again, the government established the Federal Deposit Insurance Corporation (FDIC). Up to a certain amount, the FDIC insures deposits in approved banks. In theory, your money is safe. Because of recent bank troubles, a growing number of people fear another depression. Since the government is already broke and owes trillions in debt, some assume that the FDIC would not be able to guarantee repayment of their money in the event of massive bank failures. Therefore, they keep their savings in the form of cash.
- Although it is possible for a huge economic crash in the future, we should not live in fear. If it is on the immediate horizon, take precautions; but don't be crippled with anxiety, worrying about things that may never happen. You cannot avoid every risk in life. Keeping all of your money in cash at your home may help you if the banks fail, but fire and theft may pose a greater risk than your bank's failure. Besides, you will not earn any interest on your money and will fail to keep up with inflation. Thus, your money will be worth less over time.
- While it is wise to keep some cash on hand, it is not advisable to keep your life's savings stuffed in your mattress. People who do that kind of thing rarely tell anybody where the money is hidden; and when they die, the old mattress will be sent to the town dump where it will be burned. What a waste!

NOTES

b. Savings Account

- Because you are trying to save money, you do not want instant access to all of it. Having too much cash available allows you to spend it on a whim. A savings account at your local bank can help you fight the temptation of spending your money because the cash is not in your hands. It is true that savings accounts do not earn as much interest as they used to, but that is okay. You must remember the difference between savings and investments. The purpose of your savings is to protect your money, and the purpose of investments is to see financial growth. So, it is perfectly fine to have your savings earning only a little bit of interest.
- You may find it helpful to have more than one savings account. For sure, maintain one as your emergency fund. Periodically, take money from your "Emergency Fund" envelope and deposit it into your savings account. If you are saving for a down payment on a house, you could have a separate savings account for that. People use savings accounts to save for college, cars, and large purchases. Do what works best for you.

c. Certificate of Deposit (CD)

- If you have some money that you are waiting to decide how to invest, putting it into a CD will give you higher interest than a personal savings account. It is considered a stable investment opportunity that is easily accessible. Interest is based on the length of your investment. For instance, a two-year CD will yield a slightly higher interest rate than a one-year CD. Many banks offer CDs that mature in as little as three months or up to five years.
- If you withdraw the money before the maturity date, you will lose some of the interest; but you do not lose any of the money that you deposited.

Concluding Thoughts:

✓ The Scriptures teach that wise people save money and foolish folks spend it up.

✓ Since saving is a sign of strength and God promises to give us strength, we ought to look to Him to enable us to save.

✓ Saving money provides for future needs; and with a faltering economy, we must be certain to set some funds aside.

NOTES

Review Questions

1. According to Proverbs 21:20, what kind of person spends everything and saves nothing? foolish
2. Why should we save? it is wise, it empowers, it prepares for the future, it enables giving
3. When should you begin to save? immediately, even if it is only a small amount
4. What are the most common options for saving money? cash, savings account, certificate of deposit (CD)
5. According to Proverbs 11:16, what do strong people retain? riches

---

[26] Dave Ramsey, *Financial Peace Revisited*, 274.

CHAPTER ELEVEN

MAKE WISE INVESTMENTS

Key Verse: *"But if any provide not for his own, and specially for those of his own house, he hath denied the faith, and is worse than an infidel"* (1 Timothy 5:8).

NOTES

Introductory Thoughts:

- Whether we like it or not, we have to live in the economic atmosphere of our times. In previous generations, money issues were much simpler; but now we are faced with matters we wish we never had to deal with.
- Reckless spending by politicians and an increased number of people receiving government handouts has driven our national debt to an unmanageable level.
- At some point, we are likely to face hard times. Therefore, we must take advantage of opportunities that will enable us to provide for our families in the future.
- For many, that includes establishing solid savings and investment plans.

1. THE PURPOSE OF INVESTING

- To better understand the purpose of investing, let us briefly consider the difference between saving and investing. Many see savings and investments as the same, but they are not. Knowing the difference is extremely important if you ever hope to manage your money properly. A savings plan will provide reserves for your future, while investment plans are designed to potentially grow your wealth.
- Let's review. Your savings consist of money that is readily accessible, usually in an account at your local bank. Savings are considered to be much safer than investments because they are not exposed to great risks. Although your savings earn little interest, you are less likely to lose them. Therefore, any money you want to keep protected should be

put into savings. This would definitely include money you set aside for your emergency fund. You must protect a certain portion of your money in savings.

- Investments refer to funds that you use to earn more money. An investment, therefore, is the placement of resources into a venture with prospects of obtaining a greater return. Typically, investments are exposed to greater risks than savings, but they yield higher interest rates.
- Many people invest their money to provide a nest egg for their retirement years. The idea is that money invested wisely will grow enough to stay ahead of inflation and make retirement comfortable. Those who hope to retire with what they have in savings will be disappointed in the end because their money loses value over time. When the value of the dollar drops and the cost of living rises, it means that money is not worth as much as time elapses.
- Because you need to protect some of your money, you must put a portion of it in savings for safekeeping. Because your money loses value over time, you should consider investing some of it to ensure that you are able to survive once you retire or are unable to work.
- The purpose for creating the Social Security Administration was to provide people with an investment that would guarantee a fair return upon reaching retirement. However, mismanagement of funds has nearly bankrupted the institution that so many depend upon. Therefore, it is not wise to rely upon Social Security to provide for your retirement.

2. The Potential of Investing

- While saving money has great benefits, investing money has greater potential to multiply. Many economists have constructed impressive investment models which prove the value of investing early in life.
- Illustration – Consider a very simple hypothetical example that should sufficiently illustrate the point. Bill and Steve graduated from college and entered the workforce together. Knowing he could afford the payments, Bill bought a brand-new car for $20,000 and paid it off in five years. Steve decided to buy a modest car for $5,000 and save $15,000 over the same five-year period. At the age of 27, he invested that $15,000 at 12 percent interest, compounded annually.

NOTES

With no further investments, he had $1,112,694.96 when he retired at 65. Had he waited to retire at 68, he would have had 40 percent more—$1,563,256.30. This shows how much wealth can grow as time elapses. Investing early in life allows your money to earn interest longer and to potentially multiply your investment.

- Let's go back to Bill. He spent his money on a car early in life and failed to develop the habit of saving. When he reached 37 years old, he realized that he needed to start setting money aside for retirement. He figured that the next twenty-eight years would give him ample time to save for his future. So, he put $3,000 a year into a mutual fund that earned 12 percent interest. When he retired, he had only $572,120.55. Although he invested $69,000 more than Steve, he had just over half as much as Steve when he retired because he delayed investing. In essence, his new car cost him over half a million dollars. At the time, a new car seemed like a good idea, but hindsight shows that he would have been better off saving for his golden years. This is a scenario that is repeated by many young people.
- Moses' words are quite fitting, "O that they were wise, *that* they understood this, *that* they would consider their latter end!" (Deuteronomy 32:29). Learn a huge lesson—save and invest as much as you are able, especially early in life. One day, you will be glad you did. Here's a tip: investing money on a monthly basis is easier when you set up an automatic withdrawal from your bank account. This will help ensure that you faithfully contribute to your investment.
- While there is a great potential in investing your money, there are no guarantees that it will work exactly as you plan. So, proceed with caution, and understand that you may sustain some losses along the way. Further, please do not look at the above model and think that you are entitled to be wealthy. When you start seeing dollar signs in your eyes, you better check your motives. Investing ought to be viewed as a necessity to provide for your future rather than an all-consuming focus to become rich.
- Let's not forget that many in this world do not live in economies that afford them the opportunities to invest like we have in America. It is not a God-given right to have lucrative investment plans and properties. However, if you do have such opportunities, why not take advantage of them

NOTES

to ensure that you will have money in the future to take care of your family and give to the Lord's work?

NOTES

3. The Principles for Investing

- Instead of developing a worldly view of investing, it would be wise to consider what the Scripture says. Sure there are secular principles such as "buy low and sell high," that will help you make more money. However, in this section, my aim is to consider a couple of Biblical principles that should guide our investing practices.
- What does the Bible say about making investments? Let me be clear that God gives no command in Scripture to invest money, nor does He condemn the practice. However, the Bible is filled with examples of the principle of investing. The most prominent illustration is farming. A farmer makes an investment every time he plants seeds. He takes what he currently has and hopes for a bigger return. One kernel of corn can produce hundreds of new kernels on a single ear. He knows that not every seed that is planted will grow and produce fruit, but he does not let that stop him. Furthermore, every farmer takes a risk of losing his crop due to bad weather or disease. Are farmers condemned for sowing seed and anticipating more? No. In fact, God promises a season of reaping after sowing.
- Investing is simply a means to prepare for your future. Let's consider Noah again. It was considered a great act of faith when he "prepared an ark to the saving of his house" (Hebrews 11:7). He had invested time, money, and materials to secure future deliverance. We may not be expected to build an ark, but we should follow the example of advancing our family's future.
- While there is no mention of investment portfolios and the stock market in the Bible, the principle of investing is evident. We observe it in references to sowing, growing, and reaping. Let's consider a few principles in Scripture that will guide us as we invest our money.

a. Invest for the Right Purpose

- Many invest money hoping to become rich, which is a worldly philosophy. As Christians, we must be careful not to allow the world to influence us in this manner. If you plan to invest money, you must have a Biblical basis for doing so. I believe a proper motive for investing is to be able to provide for your family in the future.

- It is a serious offence not to make provision for one's family. "But if any provide not for his own, and specially for those of his own house, he hath denied the faith, and is worse than an infidel" (1 Timothy 5:8).
- As we mentioned earlier, saving money does not keep up with inflation. So, wise investing may enable your money to grow and provide an ample amount of money when you are no longer able to work. If that allows you to provide for your family, it seems like a good choice.

b. Be a Good Steward

- In Matthew 25, Jesus used a parable involving three men who invested their master's money. Two of them invested wisely, doubling the money; but the third man, being full of fear, refused to make any investment. The application of the parable is clear. God wants us to invest our lives to make gains for His kingdom. Though the aim of the parable was not to teach men how to make monetary investments, the Lord spoke favorably of those who made wise investments and showed His disapproval of the one who failed to do so.
- Notice a couple of simple observations. First, the two men who invested were commended and rewarded for investing successfully. Second, the man who was too fearful to invest suffered loss. Instead of hearing, "Well done, good and faithful servant," he heard, "*Thou* wicked and slothful servant" (v. 23, 26). As Christians, we are stewards of what God has given to us, including our money. Doing nothing with what we have been entrusted with seems to be contrary to the whole idea of being a steward. If we are supposed to faithfully manage what we have, we must do something with it. The master told the fearful servant, "Thou oughtest therefore to have put my money to the exchangers, and *then* at my coming I should have received mine own with usury" (v. 27). The word *usury* means "interest." The master had expected the man to invest the money and earn interest with it; but because the man failed to do so, the master called him a *slothful servant.*

NOTES

- Obviously, laziness is not an acceptable character trait for any steward. Regarding our own money, it seems better to do something with it than nothing. If you choose to invest, look to God and do the best you can.

c. Be Careful of High-Risk Investments

- Investing money almost always involves risk. For that reason, some Christians think that investing money is no different than gambling. However, there is a huge difference between gambling and investing.
- George Bowman, author of *How to Succeed with Your Money*, said that gambling "is specifically aimed at gaining money from another's losses . . . On the other hand, investing provides money to help a business grow, for which the investor receives a share in the profits."[27] The goal of investing is constructive, but the practice of gambling is destructive. Participating in the stock market is certainly not the same as playing the lottery.
- Although investing involves risk, it may be more risky to be unprepared for the future. Even saving money entails risk. For instance, those who keep cash in their home risk having it stolen. Your entire life is filled with risk. Getting into a car is risky. Risk is not sinful unless your actions are foolish. The goal of those who invest money should be to limit risk, not abstain from it. While high-risk investments tend to offer the greatest short-term returns, they also leave you the most vulnerable to lose everything. Low-risk opportunities are usually safer but do not offer as much of a return.
- We would do well to heed the warning found in Proverbs 28:22, "He that hasteth to be rich *hath* an evil eye, and considereth not that poverty shall come upon him." Get-rich-quick schemes usually end in poverty. Don't let some smooth-talking "expert" convince you that you will be the exception to the rule. It is unwise to take large risks with what God has entrusted to you. To strike it rich, one has to invest in the right thing at the right time; but only a few are ever successful with "overnight" wealth.
- Since our goal is not to be rich, we must exercise caution and patience by pursuing stable investments. When

NOTES

choosing investment plans, be sure to weigh all of your options.

NOTES

4. The Possibilities for Investing

- Because the economy constantly changes, what worked a decade ago may not be as successful tomorrow. For example, some people have gotten rich by investing in real estate, and others have gone broke. Too many people are looking for a 1-2-3 plan for building wealth. If the plan fails, they point fingers at the one whose advice they followed. It is better to pray, study current investment possibilities, seek advice, and proceed with caution.
- My intentions are not to guide you to make any particular investments but rather to describe some opportunities that are available. What might work for one is no guarantee to work for another. Finding the right investment at the right time is a challenge for every investor.
- The following description of varying investment possibilities is certainly not exhaustive. My goal is to provide a brief description of the most common investment opportunities to help those who are not familiar with them, pointing out some advantages and disadvantages along the way. I hope that this cursory introduction will spark your interest to do your own research and find what will work best for you.

a. Stocks and Bonds

- Most people are familiar with the terms *stocks* and *bonds*, but the average person does not understand the difference between them. A stock is a share in a company. When companies want to raise money for their business, they may exchange shares in their company for cash. If you own stock in a company, the value of your share will increase as the company performs well. However, if the company begins to lose money, the value of the company falls, and causes your share in the company to lose value. Stocks are bought and sold through the stock market and are usually handled by brokers who trade shares on the behalf of others. When the economy does poorly and the stock market takes a negative hit, it is known as a bear market. When the market improves and stocks increase in value, it is called a bull market.

- Investment in the stock market is usually seen as a long-term proposition. Pulling your money out during a bear market may protect future loss; but once the stock rallies, you will have to pay more to get it back. However, keeping your money invested and waiting for a bull market to return can allow you to regain your money. Since the inception of the stock market, stocks have gained more than they have lost; and that is why stocks are considered to be a good long-term investment.
- If you plan to invest in the stock market, consider solid companies that share their profits with shareholders through paying dividends, allowing you to make both short-term and long-term profits. In addition to seeking professional advice, you can also research companies by the checking their *Standard & Poor's (S&P)* credit ratings. If the stock market crashes, your investment is at risk. For this reason, it is wise to diversify your investments, instead of putting it all into the stock market.
- Bonds are also offered by companies who seek to raise more capital. Rather than getting a loan from a bank, the company gets a loan from bondholders. So, when you buy a bond, you do not own a share in a company. Instead, you become a creditor to the company who offers the bond. You will be paid interest on the amount you lend the company. In most cases, it is a fixed interest rate, making it a more stable investment than the stock market. As long as the company stays in business, you will earn a set amount of interest.

b. Mutual Funds

- One of the most common ways to invest in stocks and bonds is through mutual funds. Let's face it, most people either don't know enough about the stock and bond markets, or they have little time to keep up with them. That's where mutual funds come into play. In a mutual fund, investors pool their money together to purchase securities such as stocks and bonds. The stocks and bonds are owned by the mutual fund, and investors own shares in the mutual fund. Mutual funds are operated by money managers who buy and sell securities to produce profit for the fund.

NOTES

- If you would rather have professionals with the expertise of investing manage your investment, find a mutual fund that has a proven long-term track record of making money. A little research will allow you to discover which funds have a good reputation. If you are not an expert in the stock market, a good mutual fund may be the right choice for you. Don't forget that the fund will be affected by bear and bull markets. So, be prepared to make a long-term investment and be willing to weather typical financial storms.
- The key to investing in a mutual fund is to choose the right one. When planning for retirement, Steve Brady of the Heritage Advisory Group has suggested that individuals should consider investing in growth stock mutual funds that have a track record of earning 10 to 12 percent interest over a long period of time.[28]

c. Exchange-Traded Funds (ETFs)

- ETFs are similar to mutual funds in that they group stocks and/or bonds together in a single fund. Investors who like to have a more hands-on approach often prefer ETFs because they trade more like stocks. With mutual funds, you must wait until the end of a trading day before you can trade; but ETFs can be traded at any time during the day, which might be beneficial if the markets are extremely volatile.
- Another benefit of ETFs is that they usually cost less to trade than mutual funds. Since ETFs are relatively new, it is wise to choose well-established funds to ensure that you are investing safely.

d. Real Estate

- Many people insist that real estate is the best investment. In some ways, being able to point at a house and say, "I own that," is more reassuring than hoping the stock market performs well.
- Owning property certainly has its advantages, but multitudes were greatly disappointed when the housing market crashed between 2007-2009. Home values dropped drastically, while the amount of debt owed for the homes did not. Therefore, many people owed more

NOTES

money than their home was worth, and that suddenly became a bad investment.

- When considering real estate as an investment, you must not forget that you will have to pay property taxes. High tax rates can make property an expensive investment. While owning a home is wise because it gives you a tangible asset, you may find that purchasing additional properties is less advantageous than other investments which may bring bigger returns.

NOTES

e. Precious Metals

- Silver and gold have been mainstays in every major economy since Biblical times. According to advertisers on the radio, gold and silver are the greatest investments of all time. Although the value of precious metals can increase dramatically in a struggling economy, their value can also plummet when the economy revives. Those who bought gold when it was at an all-time high in 2011, thinking the value would continue to soar, were greatly disappointed when the value plunged by over 20 percent the next year. This is not to say that it is unwise to invest in gold and silver. If you own precious metals, they will likely retain their value well in a sluggish economy; and the worse things get, the more their value may grow. Just be sure not to buy metals when prices are soaring high.
- Let's go back to the radio ads for gold and silver—many of them talk about the uncertainty of our economy and hope to get people to purchase their product out of fear. The last time I checked, Christians are not to be driven by the fear. Jesus said, "Peace I leave with you, my peace I give unto you: not as the world giveth, give I unto you. Let not your heart be troubled, neither let it be afraid" (John 14:27).
- What would happen if our economy collapses as many have speculated? Honestly, nobody knows. Some believe that gold and silver could provide great bartering power to purchase needed commodities. Others argue that tangible goods such as food and clothing would be used for bartering, believing gold and silver would have little buying power. I hope we never have to find out who is right.

- However, having a small supply of gold or silver on hand might give peace of mind if you are concerned about a failing economy. One ounce silver bars and coins are inexpensive and readily available. Because it might be difficult to gather your melted treasure from the rubble of a burnt home, be sure to have a fireproof safe if you plan to keep precious metals at your house.
- Remember that a balanced approach is important to every investment plan. If you put all of your money into metals and the economy improves instead of declines, you will regret it. An IRA account tied to gold may not produce the same income as one tied to a good mutual fund. As I said before, learn to diversify your investments.

f. IRAs

- Individual Retirement Accounts (IRAs) are used by millions of people in America. Owners of IRAs choose how they want to invest their money. Typical options include mutual funds, stocks, bonds, ETFs, CDs, and precious metals. An IRA is simply a vehicle for people to invest their money with tax advantages. Though IRAs can be invested in a variety of ways, many experts believe that those tied to reliable mutual funds typically produce the highest yields.
- There are main two types of IRAs: a traditional IRA and a Roth IRA. Contributions to traditional IRAs are not taxable. However, once you retire, the money you receive is taxable. Several years ago, the laws concerning IRAs changed, which led to the introduction of the Roth IRA. The earnings of a Roth IRA are tax-free at retirement because you pay taxes on the money that you contribute to the IRA. When the laws changed, many converted to Roth IRAs to take advantage of having tax-free earnings at retirement.
- Which one is best for you? If you think your tax-rate will be higher when you retire than they are at the time of your contributions, the Roth IRA is probably best for you.

g. 401(k) and 403(b)

- When many people hear the term *401(k)*, they are confused by its funny name. However, it is simply an

NOTES

investment opportunity offered to employees by employers, named after a part of the Internal Revenue Code. Like an IRA, it is a vehicle to invest money which offers tax advantages. A typical 401(k) plan invests in mutual funds or shares of an employer's stock.

- The 401(k) has been used by major corporations to replace pension plans. Since many companies will match employee contributions up to 3 percent of a person's income, most financial experts advise to take full advantage of it. For example, if you earn $5,000 per month, the company would match dollar for dollar what you put into the account up to $150. So, $300 is added to your account even though you only contribute $150. That is an easy way to double your money! Of course, there are rules about withdrawing money that has been invested into a 401(k). Sometimes, employers tie strings to the portion they contribute to ensure that you continue working for them, meaning that you may not be able to touch the amount your employer contributes for a certain amount of years without the risk of losing it. However, the money you contribute personally is 100 percent yours. Many people take advantage of their company's 401(k) and put money into other forms of investment in an attempt to be diversified.
- A 403(b) is similar to a 401(k) with the main difference being that it is offered by a nonprofit organization. Churches that wish to offer an investment opportunity to its employees could consider a 403(b). Likewise, missionaries may benefit from a 403(b) made available by their sending church. Both the 401(k) and 403(b) have Roth options available.

h. Eternity

- Don't make all of your investments earthly ones. When you die, you will not bring any of your possessions with you. "For we brought nothing into *this* world, *and it is* certain we can carry nothing out" (1 Timothy 6:7).
- It is wise, therefore, to have the majority of your treasures awaiting your arrival in heaven. Not all investments have guaranteed returns; but when you invest in eternity, you will have enduring treasures.

NOTES

- Jesus said, "Lay not up for yourselves treasures upon earth, where moth and rust doth corrupt, and where thieves break through and steal: But lay up for yourselves treasures in heaven, where neither moth nor rust doth corrupt, and where thieves do not break through nor steal: For where your treasure is, there will your heart be also" (Matthew 6:19-21).
- Some people worry so much about their future in this life that they neglect investing in the next life. All of your money and possessions on earth are subject to loss, but heavenly treasures endure forever. Therefore, we are foolish if we invest all of our money in temporary pursuits.
- Remember that giving to God is an investment opportunity that should never be overlooked. Not only will we have heavenly treasures, but the Lord will provide for our earthly needs as well. We will reap in heaven and in this life by investing in God's work. The Lord promises, "He which soweth sparingly shall reap also sparingly; and he which soweth bountifully shall reap also bountifully" (2 Corinthians 9:6).
- When you read, *Lay not up for yourselves treasures upon earth*, don't think it contradicts all of the teaching the Bible provides about saving money. God's Word never contradicts itself. The point of the passage is to show that earthly investments pale in comparison to heavenly ones. The Lord wants us to pray for wisdom and find a proper balance between earthly and heavenly investments.

Concluding Thoughts:

✓ The key to remember about savings and investments is diversity. A good rule to follow is, "Don't put all of your eggs in one basket." If one of the baskets falls, at least you won't lose everything! Owning a home, making use of your company's 401(k) matching investment, contributing to a Roth IRA invested in a good mutual fund, and having a small amount of precious metals has been a solid plan for many. In uncertain fiscal times, it is difficult to know which path to take; but if we seek God's guidance, He will lead us. Just be sure to keep your heavenly investments an important priority, being willing to trust God to take care of your earthly needs.

Notes

- ✓ For those who believe that investing money is foolish, remember that you are responsible to provide for your family. In America, many who fail to invest wisely end up becoming dependent on the government. If you see a problem with trusting a financially irresponsible government, perhaps you will reconsider your view of investing and begin saving some of your income on a regular basis.
- ✓ If you have not adequately planned for your future, do what you can from this time forward. I have known people who were never taught to save but had their needs met because they were generous givers. Just remember that "his [God's] mercy *endureth* for ever" (Psalm 107:1). Do your best and trust the Lord. If you have invested wisely in eternity, He will take care of you!

NOTES

REVIEW QUESTIONS

1. What is the difference between savings and investments? Savings keep money in reserve, and investments grow wealth.
2. List three Biblical principles to guide investing. invest for the right purpose, be a good steward, be careful of high-risk investments
3. How does a mutual fund differ from investing directly in the stock market? In a mutual fund, investors owns shares in a fund that is managed by money managers rather than owning shares in stocks that they manage themselves.
4. What are two basic types of IRAs? Traditional, Roth
5. What is a 401(k)? It is an investment opportunity offered by employers in which the employer matches a percentage of what the employee invests.

---

[27] Bowman, *How to Succeed with Your Money,* 21.
[28] Steve Brady is a financial advisor endorsed by Dave Ramsey. For more information about investments, visit www.heritagegroup.info.

CHAPTER TWELVE

MAKE THE MOST OF WHAT YOU HAVE

Key Verse: *"Gather up the fragments that remain, that nothing be lost"* (John 6:12).

Introductory Thoughts:

- More important than how much you have is what you do with what you have.
- Consider the example Solomon provided about the impure silver: "Take away the dross from the silver, and there shall come forth a vessel for the finer" (Proverbs 25:4). The silver was good but needed a little work. In order to produce a proper vessel, a craftsman needed to remove the impurities. Even a warehouse of impure silver would be of little use until the dross was removed. The silversmith did not need more silver, he simply had to improve the condition of the commodity that he had.
- In the same manner, God expects us to make the most of what we have.

1. MEND IT

- Follow Solomon's advice—*Take away the dross* by improving the appearance and function of what you currently have.
- For example, if you have an older car, you do not have to scrap it and buy a new one. Perhaps a little maintenance will extend its life for a season, while you save for a newer vehicle. It would be foolish to go into debt for something you do not need.
- Much of what is thrown away in our disposable society is perfectly fine.
- With a little imagination, you can get more use out of what you currently own. Try a little shoe polish on your shoes instead of buying new ones or shampooing your carpet

NOTES

instead of replacing it. A cover for a soiled couch is cheaper than purchasing new living room furniture and a mattress topper is more economical than getting a new mattress and box spring. Furthermore, a coat of paint can make many items look new!

NOTES

2. Maintain It

- If we simply take care of what we have, it will last longer. "Be thou diligent to know the state of thy flocks, *and* look well to thy herds. For riches *are* not for ever" (Proverbs 27:23-24). Because our money won't last forever, we must diligently care for our "flocks" and "herds." Failure to do so will lead to needless loss. It is amazing how many people have the mentality of "I'll just throw it away and buy another one." Proper maintenance, upkeep, and management of your possessions will enable you to get the most out of them. Thus, you will spend less money replacing things that should not need to be replaced.
- This principle applies to taking care of your body, too. If people maintained their health, they would spend less on medical bills. For example, the number of people in our nation with an obesity problem has skyrocketed, resulting in diabetes, heart disease, and many other avoidable maladies. The average American spends $898 per year on medications.[29] That is nearly $4,500 for a family of five. What could you do with a few thousand extra dollars every year? While not all health problems are avoidable, many are. Therefore, simply taking care of your health could help your budget.

3. Manage It

- Finally, let's consider the miracle of the feeding of the five thousand.
- We all remember that Jesus fed the multitude with a few loaves of bread and a couple of small fishes, teaching us that God can bless the little that we have and make it go a long way.
- Another interesting part of the account centers on the remaining fragments. "When they were filled, he said unto his disciples, Gather up the fragments that remain, that nothing be lost. Therefore they gathered *them* together, and filled twelve baskets with the fragments of the five barley

loaves, which remained over and above unto them that had eaten" (John 6:12-13). Notice how much remained after they gathered the fragments—twelve baskets full! Those small fragments added up to a great deal of provision. Always remember that conserving small portions will pay off over time. Leftovers from a couple of meals can be used to prepare another meal. Saving your spare change, instead of wasting it, can quickly turn into enough money to pay a small bill. If you follow Jesus' advice and *gather up the fragments*, you will be surprised how full your cupboards will be.

- God is not only glorified by providing miraculously but also by blessing the remaining fragments. Your part in the miracle is to manage the fragments. Isn't it exciting to put God's Word into practice and witness His power to provide? Try it today.

NOTES

Review Questions

1. List the three ways mentioned to make the most of what you have. mend it, maintain it, manage it
2. What are some examples of ways you can save money by fixing things rather than replacing them? answers will vary
3. According to Proverbs 27:23, we should *"look well"* to our possessions by taking care of them.
4. Jesus told the disciples to *"Gather up the fragments that remain"* (John 6:12).
5. How can we apply the principle of taking care of the fragments in our personal lives? answers will vary

[29] "U.S. Prescription Drug Spending Drops for First Time in 58 Years," *CBSnews.com*, last modified May 9, 2013, http://www.cbsnews.com/news/us-prescription-drug-spending-drops-for-first-time-in-58-years/.

Chapter Thirteen

Reduce Spending

Key Verse: *"And every man that striveth for the mastery is temperate in all things"* (1 Corinthians 9:25).

Introductory Thoughts:

- When you need to improve your financial situation, you either have to make more money or cut spending.
- While we would all like to earn more money, most of us do not control the payroll department at work. So, if you can't earn more, you will have to settle for spending less. In a sense, if you learn how to reduce your spending, it is like giving yourself a raise. After all, the less you spend the more you will have.

1. Reasons to Cut Spending

- Have you ever wondered why rich people tend to have money? The reason is because they don't spend it all! Why not put into practice the strategy of many rich people?
- By cutting spending, you will have more money, too. While you may not become rich, you will certainly improve your financial situation.
- Before considering some practical ways to cut spending, let's remember a few important reasons to reduce spending.

a. Stuff Doesn't Satisfy

- Somehow we have bought into the world's philosophy that material possessions bring happiness. Jesus said that "a man's life consisteth not in the abundance of the things which he possesseth" (Luke 12:15). There is much more to life than accumulating stuff.
- Buying something new does not quench our thirst for more stuff. For example, the guy who just bought a new car will only be satisfied until the new model comes out. No matter how much we think our dream purchase will

Notes

please us, it won't be long until we crave something else. That's human nature.
- Getting new stuff creates another problem—more stuff. For instance, buying a new laptop often leads to other purchases: updated software, a new case, and all of the "I-got-to-have" accessories.

b. Debt Is Reduced

- There's that terrible word again—debt. Here is a simple step to reduce debt: reduce spending. You can avoid fees and interest by refusing to buy things you can live without. If for no other reason, we ought to cut spending so that we can either get out of debt or prevent ourselves from going into it.
- Perhaps you are in debt and currently have no extra money available to pay off that debt. If you could find a way to save $150 per month, you would have $150 to pay toward that looming debt. By following some of the suggestions that follow in this chapter, many people could slash their spending by hundreds every month. Are you ready to get serious about paying off your outstanding debt? If so, determine to reduce your spending.

c. Savings Are Increased

- Controlling your spending not only allows you to conquer debt, it enables you to save for future needs. If you spend money on something you don't need today, you will have less for the necessities of tomorrow. Stop living for the present.
- Some people complain, "I don't have any extra money that I can put in savings." Once they reduce their spending, they will have money to save for future emergencies and invest for retirement.

2. Ways to Cut Spending

- If you are convinced about the need to cut back on expenses, it's time to get started doing it. Here are some tips that will help you get the most out of your money.

NOTES

NOTES

a. Remember That Spending Is Not the Same as Saving

- Most advertisers try to reassure you that you will save money by purchasing their product. We have all heard slogans like, "Save big money!" However, you never save money by spending it.
- Retailers have successfully redefined the word *save*. You may be spending less money, but you certainly are not saving anything. If you buy something just because it is on sale, you spent money you would not have otherwise spent. For example, a lady decided to buy some new clothes that were greatly discounted. At the bottom of the sales receipt, it said that she saved $97 while only spending $22. The truth is that she never would have bought the clothes at full price. Because the clothes cost $22, she did not save money, she spent $22.
- Sales events cause people to buy items they normally would not buy. Getting a good deal on something you do not need is never a good deal. Spending $1 on a useless $5 item is a waste of $1, not a savings of $4. Countless arguments arise in marriages over needless spending. One spouse says, "Why did you buy that piece of junk?" The other responds, "It was on sale!" When you are on a tight budget, every purchase must be wise.
- While it is wise to purchase items that you need when they are on sale, it is silliness to buy things just because they are drastically reduced in price. Unfortunately, we all have junk lying around the house, proving that getting a good deal on worthless stuff is not such a good deal. If you have a problem resisting bargains, stay out of the clearance aisle!

b. Think in Terms of Hours at Work

- Many of your waking hours are spent at work and driving to and from work. Because you need to provide for your family, you are willing to exchange a huge part of your life for money. However, if you get little in exchange for the time you spend at work, you would think that it was not worth it. When you buy something, you are not merely spending money—you are spending part of your life. If you begin to think in terms of how many hours it takes to earn the money you spend, you may start spending differently. Let's say that you want to buy a watch. So, you go to the store and look at a Timex and a Rolex. Although you would really like the Rolex, you begin to calculate how much time it would take to acquire it. Soon, you realize that working for a couple hours for a Timex is better than spending over a week of your life working just to have a Rolex on your wrist.

- By converting purchases into hours spent at work, you will find yourself being more careful about how you spend the money you work so hard to earn. After all, some items are not worth exchanging your life to get. In reality, to waste money is to waste part of your life.

c. Buy with Cash

- We looked at the pros and cons of using credit cards in a previous chapter. It is worth revisiting the subject briefly as we discuss the topic of cutting spending. If you want to reduce expenditures, try making all of your everyday purchases using cash. Research shows that people who purchase using credit tend to spend up to 20 percent more than those who shop with cash.[30] So, simply avoiding credit cards will help you spend less. Psychologically, it is easier to sign a piece of paper than it is to hand over your hard-earned money. When you go shopping with cash, you are more in control of your spending because credit makes it very easy to buy now and try to figure out how to pay later. So, if you want to cut spending, try using cash for your purchases. You might be amazed at how much incidental spending would be eliminated.
- Additionally, by going to the "cash only" method, you will be forced to actually pull the money from an existing envelope in order to make each purchase. This not only prevents overspending but causes you to evaluate each purchase to determine if it is absolutely necessary.

d. Conserve at Home

- Utility bills can cost a small fortune, accounting for a large part of your monthly expenditures.
- Turning the thermostat down a couple of degrees in the winter and turning it up a little in the summer will cut your heating and air conditioning expenses. Another way to save on utilities is to close air vents and doors to rooms

NOTES

that are unoccupied. Switching off lights when you leave a room can also really add up to savings. Stop playing a stereo to an empty room and hibernate your computer when not working on it. To save on your water bill, take shorter showers and wait until you have enough laundry for a full load.

- Once you learn to budget your money properly, you will begin to accumulate some cash in your envelopes. Instead of spending the money on a "dream" kitchen, use it for more practical renovations that lead to greater energy efficiency. For instance, replacing drafty windows can reduce your heating bill. When you cut spending in other areas, you will eventually have enough to build your "dream" kitchen.

e. Plan for Christmas

- Every year, you know it is coming! In fact, Christmas lands on the same date every year. So, why do people get taken off guard? They fail to plan. Instead of enjoying the season, people are filled with frustration because they are not prepared for Christmas shopping.
- In your budget, you should have an envelope marked *Gifts*. Throughout the year, you will see things on sale; and when you see a great deal, you can buy the gifts that you want to give at Christmas time. When people fail to budget their money, they are unable to purchase the gifts that they would like to buy for their loved ones. Then, feeling guilty, they buy them anyway and go into debt. Remember, you cannot spend money that you do not have; and that means you cannot buy things that are not budgeted. The spirit of Christmas is giving, not going into debt! Give only what you can afford to give and stay out of debt.

f. Spend Fifteen Minutes or Less

- Shop around for cheaper car insurance. You may be surprised at how much you can slash your insurance payment. Do your homework, and get quotes from a few of the top-rated insurance companies. Depending on the value of your vehicle, a savings of 10-15 percent could cut your premiums by hundreds of dollars.

NOTES

- One word of caution—be sure that you are comparing apples with apples. Just because one company offers a lower premium does not guarantee it is a better deal. For instance, Company A may offer you a lower rate than Company B but may offer less benefits should you file a claim.
- Another way to save money on insurance is by grouping multiple policies with one insurance company. The term in the insurance industry for this is a *multiline discount.* Typically, those who insure their home and automobiles qualify for reduced premiums.

g. Change Your Cell Phone Plan

- Millions of Americans spend hundreds of dollars a month on cellular phone service. A couple of years ago, I met a family that spent over $400 per month! If you need to trim expenses, consider switching to a pre-paid plan. Although the latest phone models are not always available, you can still find good phones that will meet your needs and allow you to dramatically cut spending. In many cases, it is possible to save up to 50 percent on your monthly expenses. Just think what you could do with the extra money!
- Pre-paid companies like Total Wireless and Straight Talk often allow you to use your current phone, transfer your number, and enjoy unlimited talk, text, and data at a fraction of the cost of competitors. Shop around for plans offered by such providers. You may also consider Republic Wireless which offers incredibly low rates by utilizing Wi-Fi connections when possible to make phone calls.

h. Throw Out the TV

- We could list a number of reasons to get rid of your television, but one that is often overlooked is the financial drain it imposes on a family's budget. Believe it or not, owning a television is not a necessity in life. When people cannot make ends meet, they never think about giving up their TV, regardless of how much money they waste on monthly service charges. Even if they have to eat Ramen noodles every night, they wouldn't give up their "right" to TV ownership.

NOTES

- A TV-free family will save more than just monthly charges. They will not fall prey to the "bigger and better screen" sales pitch made by the electronic industry. Many people upgrade their televisions every couple of years just to have the latest technology. Households can literally save hundreds of dollars a year by simply not having a television.

i. Pack a Lunch and Make a Pot of Coffee

- Convenience is king in our culture. People would rather spend a "little extra" to buy a lunch or get a coffee at their favorite coffee shop. The truth is that it adds up to far more than a little extra. Even grabbing fast food just twice a week will cost you cost you around $50 per month. Getting a coffee every morning really drains the wallet, too.
- Take a few extra minutes every morning to pack a lunch. Try making a sandwich, preparing a salad, or bringing leftovers to work. By making a weekly plan, you can add variety to your lunches and save lots of money in the process. Besides, you can eat healthier by packing food that is not loaded with grease, calories, and additives. By eating food that is better for your body, you will end up saving money on medical bills in the future. So, get your pen ready and start planning your budget-friendly lunches!
- I know that some of you are coffee connoisseurs, but a package of coffee that can last an entire month costs the same as two cups of your fancy blends at the coffee shop. Even if "America runs on Dunkin'™," they could do it cheaper by purchasing a bag of their coffee and brewing it at home.[31] Not only will you save money on coffee, you will also avoid the temptation to buy donuts, pastries, and breakfast items while stopping to get coffee. If cutting back on things you like seems too radical, forget about saving money.

j. Limit Dining Out

- It used to be that going to a nice restaurant was a special occasion. Not so anymore. Dining out has grown to be a common practice in our society. Even during our recent economic recession, many restaurants still had full

NOTES

parking lots. Unfortunately, we have grown accustomed to living in an affluent nation, causing us to take for granted such luxuries as dining out. As a child, just going to McDonald's was a special treat for our family. In fact, I can only remember going out to one nice restaurant as a family while growing up. It is not that my parents neglected family time. We simply did other things that did not require spending a lot of cash. Values have changed in our society, and too much emphasis has been placed on living luxuriously.

- A family of five will easily spend over $50 at a family restaurant. Those who eat out once a week will spend over $200 a month! If you are trying to cut spending, this is a great place to start. Reduce the number of times you dine out. Perhaps you will cut a few pounds in the process, too.
- To save on dining out, let's consider a few tips. First, go to less expensive restaurants. You can buy a good steak without spending $50. Second, arrive at the restaurant before they switch to the more expensive dinner menu. Lunchtime meals are almost always cheaper. Third, order a glass of water instead of a soft drink. A family of four will save over $10 by getting water. If you insist on drinking something with flavor, ask for a slice of lemon in your water and add sweetener from the little packets at the table—it makes tasty lemonade. Fourth, share a meal. At some restaurants, the portions are large enough to split. Fifth, skip desert. You probably don't need the extra calories anyway. Sixth, look for BOGO free coupons online. Many family restaurants offer special discounts via weekly emails. Seventh, join birthday clubs. Some chain restaurants will send a coupon for a free meal on your child's birthday. Eighth, complete online surveys when they offer you a free product.

k. Grow It

- Eating fresh vegetables is healthy for you, but it can be expensive. Planting a small garden can be just the solution. Having a garden not only gives you something to do as a family, it will also save you some cash. When you have an abundance of crops, freeze some for the coming months when it is too cold to have a garden.

NOTES

l. Stay at Home

- Have you ever been surprised at how much you spent during a trip to the store? You went out to buy just one thing; but by the time you hit the checkout line, your cart was half full. If you cannot control your spending, you would save a lot of money by simply staying at home!

m. Negotiate Medical Bills

- Unfortunately, health problems often result in financial problems. Even with health insurance, high deductibles and co-pays can lead to huge medical bills. Because hospitals and healthcare providers want to be paid as quickly as possible, they usually give big discounts if you offer to pay off the bill with cash. For instance, Bob owes $2,000 to a hospital. Because he has saved money in an envelope for medical expenses, Bob is able to call the hospital and offer to pay off the bill immediately if they agree to reduce the bill to $1,500. Money talks! If you do not have insurance, many providers will give you big discounts if you agree to pay cash at the time of service. You can save thousands of dollars by negotiating your medical bills.
- Many hospitals offer financial assistance through grants they receive. Even if you think you may not qualify, you might be surprised. One particular university hospital allows a person to earn up to $150,000 annually and still qualify for assistance. Even if your bill is reduced by a small percentage, it will help you pay it off faster.

n. Stay Healthy

- Instead of spending large amounts of money on medical expenses, try to avoid them. Just about every time I go shopping at a place like Wal-Mart, I see people who are terribly overweight and suffering from serious medical conditions. It motivates me to take care of myself and cut back on bad food items.
- By watching what we eat and exercising regularly, we can avoid many health problems and the costs that are associated with them. Developing the simple habit of brushing your teeth after meals and flossing once a day can save thousands of dollars on trips to the dentist. I'm not sure which hurts more—getting a root canal or paying

NOTES

for it! Why not just take better care of yourself? Being unhealthy adds many costs to your life: doctor's bills, prescriptions, supplements, medical devices, surgeries, physical therapy, etc. On top of that, the more your health insurance has to pay toward your medical bills, the higher your insurance premiums will become. All of this can add up to a large portion of your monthly budget. So, do your best to stay fit!

- Have you ever considered that your health directly affects your ability to work and make money? If you are unhealthy, you will not be able to work as much in a week, and that will be reflected in your paycheck. Further, poor health can limit the number of years you have in the work force, making it more difficult to plan for retirement. If you say you are too busy to exercise and maintain a proper diet, you will reduce the number of productive years of your life. Is that what you want?

o. Plan Your Vacations Wisely

- It is amazing how much money could be saved if people took time to plan their vacations. When you think of it, a family vacation is one of biggest "purchases" that you will make during the year. If you had $1,000 to spend on a computer, you would shop around and find the best deal possible. Why not treat your vacation the same way?

1) *Make a budget.*

- Determine how much money you have to spend and make a budget for your trip. Be sure to include travel (fuel or airfare), lodging, meals, and activities. Decide which parts of the budget are most important to you. For instance, if you insist on staying at a nice hotel, you will have less to spend on meals and activities. Once you decide how much you have to spend, you can decide where you want to go. If you do not have enough money in the budget to go on a dream vacation, take a shorter, cheaper vacation in order to save for the one you really want.

2) *Decide your mode of transportation.*

- Determine if it is cheaper to drive or fly to your destination. You may be surprised that flying can sometimes be cheaper. Airlines often have fare wars

NOTES

or offer special discounts. As mentioned before in an earlier chapter, accumulating airline miles with a credit card can provide you with free flights. You can't get any cheaper than free!

3) ***Plan early.***
   - Be sure to plan early. The later you wait to make reservations, the more you are likely to pay. This is especially true when flying. Airlines have a limited amount of economy fares; and when they sell out, you will have to pay much more. You also need to reserve your lodging as far in advance as possible. Some places have a limited number of hotels available, and the cheaper ones fill up quickly. If you have your heart set on going to a particular area and delay in making reservations, you will have to pay much more for lodging. It is wise to make reservations about six months in advance.
4) ***Eat cheaply.***
   - Another great way to reduce spending is to plan economical meals. Let's face it, eating out is not cheap; and if you dine at restaurants three times a day on a ten-day trip, you are going to spend a small fortune. First, try to book hotel rooms that offer free breakfast. That alone can cut your food budget by one third. If your hotel does not offer free breakfast, bring some packets of instant oatmeal and granola bars. When eating at fast food restaurants, buy items off the value menu. By packing a crock pot, you can start a simple meal in the morning and have it ready by the time you get back to your hotel room in the evening.[32] Just be sure to leave the crock pot on a safe surface! When traveling, we often purchase deli meat, nice bread, lettuce, and a couple of tomatoes. We find that making our own sandwiches is far better than eating greasy fast food. It is cheaper, better tasting, and healthier. Those sandwiches are a highlight of our trips. Of course, a loaf of bread and jars of peanut butter and jelly make a quick, inexpensive lunch meal.
5) ***Get the most out of eating out.***
   - If you plan on splurging on a few nice meals, remember that lunch menus usually are much cheaper

NOTES

than dinner menus. By eating a large lunch, you will normally only need a small meal or light snack in the evening. One last tip about saving on food—buy snacks and drinks at a grocery store rather than gas stations and convenience stores. You can purchase a whole case of water at a grocery store for the price you pay for two bottles at a convenience store. While we are discussing water, not only is it better for you than soda pop, it is cheaper. Numerous drink mixes are on the market that you can add to bottled water, giving your taste buds something a little sweet. Need a cold drink? Fill a small cooler with ice at the hotel before you heading out for the day.

6) ***Choose off-season travel dates.***
   - If possible, plan your vacation during non-peak times. Taking a trip in spring or fall is usually cheaper than during the summer season when the demand is high. Oh yes, the law of supply and demand applies to vacations, too. Why not capitalize on capitalism by traveling in the off season?

7) ***Maintain self-control.***
   - Finally, avoid the "I'm-on-vacation" mind-set. People tend to relax more than just their body while vacationing—they relax their self-control. It is easy to indulge and overspend, justifying it because of a "once-in-a-lifetime" opportunity. Make your budget and stick to it.

NOTES

Review Questions

1. What are three reasons to cut spending? stuff does not satisfy, debt is reduced, savings are increased
2. What is meant by "thinking in terms of hours at work"? Think about how many hours you must work to earn enough to purchase what you want. This will cause you to spend more carefully.
3. What are some ways to conserve at home? cut back on heat, A/C, lights, water usage, renovations
4. How can staying healthy save you money? answers will vary
5. What are some things to consider when planning a vacation? budget, transportation, early planning, eating cheaply, travel dates, self-control

---

[30] Larry Burkett, *Get a Grip on Your Money* (Gainesville: Christian Financial Concepts, Inc., 1996), 32.
[31] *America Runs on Dunkin'* is a trademark of Dunkin' Donuts USA, Inc.
[32] Steve Economides and Annette Economides, *America's Cheapest Family Gets You Right on the Money* (New York: Three Rivers Press, 2007), 210.

Chapter Fourteen

Shop Wisely

Key Verse: *"A gracious woman retaineth honour: and strong men retain riches"* (Proverbs 11:16).

Introductory Thoughts:

- The above verse reveals much about a person's character. The key word in the verse is *retain.* Gracious women maintain honor, and strong men hang on to their money. When applied to shopping, it is good to keep your dignity and cash by not getting ripped off.
- It is no mistake that this chapter follows the one about reducing spending. If you want to cut spending, you need to learn to shop wisely. Whether shopping for small or large items, you must look for ways to save money. Here are a few pointers.

1. Change Your Thinking

a. Rethink Sales Events

- What is the purpose of a sales event—to save you money or to get you to spend money? Although businesses want you to think that you are saving money, they are actually trying to lure you to spend it. You must remember that the retail world is not out to help you. Stores want to make money. As a consumer, you must learn to be in the driver's seat.
- Most of us see a sales ad and say something like, "Wow! That's a good deal. I better run to the store and get that." If you had never seen the advertisement, you would not be in a hurry to get to the store. Too often, we buy things just because they are on sale, regardless of whether we need them or not.
- Beware of deceptive advertising. For example, "deep discounts" do not always equal great deals. Too often,

Notes

retailers overinflate their original prices, making sale prices seem unbelievably generous. In many cases the "great" sale price is the same as a competitor's everyday price. Be sure that the item you want to purchase is actually worth the price that is marked, regardless of how much it has been "discounted."

- Sales are horrible things when they tempt you to buy things that you do not need. Sales are wonderful things when they allow you to spend less money on items that you already plan to buy. Learn to look at sales events as a tool to accomplish your financial goals, and refuse to allow them to lead to needless spending.

b. Be Patient

- We've all heard the famous saying—"Haste makes waste." Quick decisions lead to unnecessary spending. I remember a time that I needed some new white dress shirts. While at a store, I saw a good brand on sale; but the price was still a little higher than I wanted to pay. So, I decided to wait. My patience paid off because I got two new dress shirts for free! How? I received a coupon in the mail which gave $50 off a purchase of $50 or more. While redeeming this giveaway, I asked the salesclerk why the company sent out coupons like that. She told me that the store sends those coupons to lure infrequent shoppers back to the store. I am glad that I did not take matters into my own hands and spend money that I did not have to buy what God had planned to give me.
- Being patient not only allows you to wait upon the Lord's timing, it also enables you to shop around for better bargains. How many times have you bought something, only to find it for a better price in the next store you entered? "For ye have need of patience" (Hebrews 10:36).
- A good practice to follow, especially on big purchases, is to wait 24-48 hours before making a final decision. This gives you time to think it over, pray about it, crunch the numbers, and consult your spouse's opinion. We tend to be fine with the first three, but ask our spouse? Seriously, if you hesitate talking about a purchase to your mate, it is a good indication that maybe you should not buy it.

NOTES

c. Avoid Paying Full Price

- Illustration – Imagine that Brad wants to purchase a new computer. He has money set aside for it in his budget, but it is not on sale. Because he wants it so badly, he does not wait for it to go on sale and pays full price. Two weeks later, the computer is marked down by $100. Brad realizes that his impatience just cost him a chunk of money. Have you ever found yourself in a similar situation?
- If you want to reduce spending, purpose to wait until you can find items on sale before purchasing. "My soul, wait thou only upon God; for my expectation *is* from him" (Psalm 62:5). If you are convinced that God wants you to have something, why not ask Him to help you find it for a lower price? You may say, "Is God interested in how I spend my money?" Definitely! The principle of waiting on God can apply to every area of our lives.
- Many people are far too impatient when it comes to buying things. They know what they want and want it immediately. Despite working long hours to earn their money, they needlessly waste it by failing to shop around for good deals. Even if you do not like purchasing items online, you can still compare prices to find the best deal. Then, you can go to the store that offers the lowest price and buy the desired item.
- Another way to avoid paying full price is to ask for a discount. On larger purchases, you can often shop around and ask competitors if they can beat another store's price. It never hurts to ask. You may be surprised to find that some prices are negotiable.
- Using coupons for everyday items can lead to significant savings. In addition to checking the Sunday paper for coupons, check online for weekly coupons at websites such as Coupons.com. If you shop on the Internet, search for a coupon code online before checking out. One of the most popular sites which lists coupon codes is Retailmenot.com. It is not uncommon to find coupon codes that enable you to save 20 percent off your entire purchase.
- If you do not need a brand-new item, try shopping at pawn shops. People who need quick cash often sell possessions that are perfectly fine. You can find tools,

NOTES

bikes, small appliances, jewelry, and electronic devices at a fraction of the cost.

- Finally, don't forget to wait for big sales events such as Black Friday and Cyber Monday. Some of the biggest sales of the year occur just before Christmas. So, save your money and wait for the big sale. Don't forget that you can find many items on sale for 50 percent off or more just after Christmas. If you are patient, you can usually find a good bargain.

d. Do Your Homework

- Buyer's regret is real. Have you ever said, "I wish I had never bought that stupid thing"? Any time you plan on making a big purchase, spend some time researching your available options. Check *Consumer Reports*, read product reviews, and talk to people you know who own what you are interested in purchasing. You can spare yourself a lot of grief by taking heed to the advice of experts or by learning from the mistakes of others.

2. Make a Plan

a. Stop Impulse Buying

- It is an amazing phenomenon—as you walk down the aisle of your favorite store, an item on the shelf jumps into your arms and says, "Buy me." Well, maybe you help it jump a little. The truth is that things catch our eye while we are out shopping, and we purchase things on the spur of the moment.
- Marketing involves more than just sending out sales flyers and flooding the airwaves with clever ads. People are paid huge salaries to invent ways to grab your attention while you are shopping. End displays, discount shelves, in-store product videos, and items at the checkout counter are carefully chosen and placed to get you to spend money impulsively.
- Impulses are powerful emotions. However, like other emotions, they do not have to be followed. A Christian should not be controlled by feelings. When a person cannot control their feelings, in this case spending uncontrollably, he is obviously walking contrary to God's plan for his life. Impulse buying is actually a spiritual

Notes

problem. Because the Spirit of God produces temperance (self-control), we know that anytime we demonstrate a lack of self-control is a sign that we are not filled with the Spirit (Galatians 5:22-23). Therefore, submitting to the Spirit of God will actually help you control your spending!

- A couple of practical ideas can also be of assistance. First, go to the store with a shopping list. Tell yourself, "Only buy what's on the list, no matter how good the deal is." If you are trying to save money, you know what you need and must not let others convince you what to buy through marketing ploys. So, shop with purpose. Second, never give in to a pushy salesman. How many times have we heard, "This is such a good sale, and I really don't know how long these items will stay on the shelf. When they're gone, they're gone"? Because you don't want to miss such a good deal, you end up buying something that was not an immediate need. Third, wait for a day or two before making a large purchase. This will give you time to pray about it, discuss the matter with someone who is objective, and come to a rational decision.

b. Buy Generics

- I will be the first one to admit that not all store brand items taste the same as name brand foods. However, many products do taste the same, and a few even taste better. When you find that you cannot do without your favorite product, wait until it goes on sale and stock up.
- When it comes to buying medicine, always check for generics. You can save hundreds of dollars per year on prescription medications by simply asking for a generic brand. Store brand over-the-counter medicines that have the same ingredients as name brand products cost a fraction of the price. By taking the time to carefully read the labels, you can cut your expenses.
- Occasionally, doctors prescribe medicine that is also available over the counter. For instance, if you are prescribed 800 mg of ibuprofen, you do not need to pay more by filling the prescription at the pharmacy. Since ibuprofen is available over the counter, taking four 200 mg tablets would equal one 800 mg pill prescribed by the

NOTES

doctor. By following the dosage instructions provided by your doctor, you can enjoy the same treatment for a fraction of the cost. However, if your health insurance pays for prescription medicine, you might spend less by having the prescription filled and submitting it to your insurance company. (Note: Always check with your doctor to ensure that over the counter medicine is actually compatible with what has been prescribed.)

NOTES

c. Buy in Bulk

- Generally speaking, the more you buy of a product, the better deal you get. For instance, a small package of oatmeal will cost more per ounce than a 50 lb. bag of it. Some grocery stores have tags on their shelves that list the price per ounce for the product. By buying a little extra of a product that you know you will use in the future, you can pay less.
- Stores like Costco and Sam's Club allow you to save money by buying larger quantities. Just remember that not everything is a good deal. In some cases, you may pay more. So, always do your homework. Most warehouse stores charge an annual membership; but if you shop often enough, it is usually worth it.

d. Shop at Discount Grocery Outlets

- Name brand products at discount prices are in abundance at grocery outlets. Whether a box is slightly crushed or a can is dented, the food still tastes the same. Who cares what the package looks like on the outside! With the money you save on groceries, you can go out to eat with your spouse or save for a getaway.
- Many items at discount outlets are either near or just past the expiration date. In most cases, the food is perfectly fine if you plan on using it in the near future. Although some people worry about buying products that will soon be out of date, there is a good rule to follow. Learn the difference between "Best Before" and "Use By" on the label. Items marked "Best Before" are only guaranteed up to the suggested date but are normally still good after that date. Exercise more caution when products are labeled "Use By" because they are more prone to spoil shortly after the expiration date.

e. Shop at Thrift Stores

- So much of what you need is available at thrift stores: clothes, shoes, kitchen items, and furniture. New and like-new clothes can be purchased at thrift stores, allowing you to save a fortune on your wardrobe. Let others pay big money for designer items, and then you can buy them for a fraction of the cost when they get tired of them! For example, I have found ties in excellent condition for a dollar or two at thrift stores.
- Those who have children know how quickly they outgrow their clothes. You can get much more for your money by buying secondhand clothing. Instead of buying one new outfit, you can buy a few like-new ones at a thrift store. The same goes for shoes. Since many children outgrow their shoes before they outwear them, they get rid of them; and just the right pair may be waiting on the shelf for your child.
- Every day, people find deals that are too good to be true. A friend of mine bought an inkjet printer that was still in the box, and in the box was a brand-new digital camera. Whether you need some classical music CDs, games, picture frames, sports equipment, an alarm clock, or kitchen decorations, chances are that one of your local thrift stores has something that you are looking for. Many stores have special sale days, offering 50 percent off everything in the store. Why not take an afternoon and get to a few thrift stores in your area?

f. Be Wise at Yard Sales

- Some excellent deals can be found at yard sales. If you are looking for items for children, this can be a great place to shop. People spoil their children and think they are good parents because they buy expensive clothes, strollers, playpens, highchairs, and car seats. Let someone else pay the top dollar and enjoy the items for pennies on the dollar. Other things that can be good deals at a yard sale are small appliances, furniture, and fitness equipment. However, you must remember what we discussed earlier—you don't save money by spending. If you are trying to cut spending, you should not be shopping at every yard sale that you pass.

NOTES

- Shopping at yard sales is kind of a hobby to some people. They are "professional" deal-getters, purchasing all sorts of things they do not need for bargain prices.
- Just because something is a good deal does not mean you should buy it. Even if an item is something you could use, you should not buy it if you do not have money in your budget to pay for it.
- When you shop at yard sales, go with an idea of what you need or set a limit on what you will spend. Be sure not to buy things that you do not need. The old saying goes like this—one man's junk is another man's treasure. How much treasured junk do you have in your house?

g. Buy Quality Merchandise

- Much spending is unwise. You never save money when you buy inferior merchandise. Purchasing low-quality products usually means that they will either not do the job properly or will not stand the test of time. In the long run, you will spend more by getting cheap stuff because of having to replace it sooner.
- A good rule of thumb to follow is to purchase products that are in the middle price range. When you buy the least expensive item, you often get a product that is often substandard, while the most expensive items usually have a lot of bells and whistles that you can do without.

h. Buy Conservative Clothing

- Conservative patterns and colors almost never go out of style. If you like to look trendy, you will pay for it. Not only are current fashions more expensive, they also pass quickly. Some styles only last a few months. In order to stay looking "chic," you will have to continually spend money; but if you dress conservatively, your wardrobe will last much longer.

i. Learn How to Shop for a Car

- With the exception of purchasing a home, buying a car is probably the biggest purchase you will make. It makes sense to do your homework, and save as much as possible. I enjoy shopping for cars and consider it a challenge to get the best deal possible. Learning a few

NOTES

basics has allowed me to get some great buys over the years. Here are a few tips:

NOTES

1) ***Determine what you can afford.*** Decide how much money you plan to spend on a vehicle. As mentioned earlier, it is best to save money and purchase your car with cash. Because vehicles depreciate so quickly in value, a loan can leave you owing more money than the car is worth. Besides, paying interest on something that loses value is not wise. Once you decide how much you have to spend on a car, stick to your budget. You can be sure that you will see a car that you really want for what seems like only a little more money, but resist the urge to overcommit yourself.
2) ***Avoid new cars.*** Driving the latest model is appealing to most of us, but buying new is almost never a good value. (Remember that this section of the book is about spending less. So, if you have enough money to buy a new car with cash, go ahead and enjoy it.) New cars depreciate more than used cars and typically lose thousands of dollars the moment you take possession of them. If you insist on buying a new car, go to several dealers and get written quotes of their best offer. Then, take the best quote to other dealers and ask if they are able to beat the price. This takes time, but it can literally save you thousands of dollars.
3) ***Beware of new car ads.*** I have seen new cars advertised for less money than used cars. If a deal is absolutely unbelievable, don't believe it. The price listed in the newspaper often reflects every imaginable discount and rebate, most of which you do not qualify to receive. When you get to the dealership and are ready to buy, the salesman gives you the real price. Such dealers figure that once you have committed to buy, you will be willing to spend more than you planned. It is deceitful and dishonest. Stay clear of these kinds of dealers.
4) ***Consider certified pre-owned vehicles.*** In many cases, cars that are factory certified come with better warranties than new cars. These vehicles typically have low miles and may even have the new car smell! Because the previous owner suffered the initial dramatic depreciation,

you get a like-new car with a better warranty for thousands less. It is a great alternative to buying new.

5) ***Investigate used cars.*** You always run a risk when you buy a used car—it is part of the territory. However, buying from reliable sources can bring peace of mind. Avoid doing business with shady characters that advertise in the newspaper or online. If it seems too good to be true, it probably is. Local dealers may charge a little more than a private sale, but their reputation is on the line so they are usually careful not to intentionally sell a "lemon." By taking the following steps, you can improve the chances of getting a reliable used car.
   a) Look at the CARFAX report. This will provide a history of the vehicle that will assist in your decision making. It will tell you the number of owners, type of owners (personal, rental, or corporate), title problems, and mileage records. If the car was involved in a reported accident, details of the accident may be recorded in the report. If the car was serviced by a dealer, the service records will be indicated. Here's the best type of used vehicle to purchase: one owner, no accidents, low mileage, clear title, and well maintained. Best of all, most dealers allow you to view the CARFAX for free through their website. If you are checking cars sold by individuals, you will have to pay for each CARFAX report.
   b) Check the blue book value. By going to KBB.com, you can get an accurate idea of what you should expect to pay for a used car. Remember that there are two different categories listed: private sale or dealership. If you buy from a dealer, expect to pay more than you would in a private sale. If I buy from a dealer, I always check what the value is for a private sale. Why? I do not want to pay more for a car than I can sell it for. Always try to buy your car close to or under the private sale book value. If you can manage to do that, you will get a good deal.
   c) Take a peek in the glove box. There are two good reasons to check the glove box: look for odometer discrepancies and check for maintenance records. If the actual mileage of a vehicle is different from the odometer (which may legitimately occur if part of the

NOTES

instrument panel has been replaced), a sticker is placed in the glove box to provide the details. Also, by checking for maintenance records, you can find out a lot about the vehicle. If you find a receipt for a rebuilt transmission, you know that the car may soon have more trouble. However, you may find some good news. For example, after checking the glove box of a car I was interested in buying, I found a detailed notebook with a complete service record, including everything from oil changes, tire rotations, and wiper blade replacements. The car was well maintained, and I bought it!

d) Have it checked by a mechanic. If you know someone who is a mechanic, bring him with you to look at the car before you buy it. He can spot things that you may not see.

e) Look at the tires. If the tires are excessively worn, negotiate for a lower price for the car. You do not want to have to buy four new tires shortly after you purchase a car.

f) Be thorough, try to get a good deal, but don't be rude. Salesmen have to earn a living, too. If they cannot give you the price you want, find another car. Don't allow covetousness to cause you to ruin your testimony.

6) *Think twice before trading in your car.*

- Car dealers are in business to make money, and they make more money when you trade in your car. Here's how it works. They offer you less than your car is worth, mark it up dramatically, and resell it. If you sell your older car through a private sale, you will get much more money for it.
- Illustration – Dave Olson explains, "One time while buying a car, I was asked by the salesman if I planned on trading in my other vehicle. I had already looked up my car's value and thought it would be interesting to see what the dealer would offer me for the car. Their offer confirmed what I already knew—I would lose money by trading it. I ended up selling the car privately for more than 50 percent over what I was offered."

NOTES

- Many dealers are good at using marketing terms to convince you to trade in your vehicle. For instance, they may advertise that they pay "fair market price" for trade-ins. That sounds good, but what does that mean? It all depends upon how a dealer defines the term. In some cases, "fair market price" is quite different from the blue book value. In fact, it can be much lower, causing us to wonder why they call it fair.
- Not all cars that are accepted as trade-ins are worth reselling. So, dealers typically offer the price they can recapture at an auction. This allows them to accept a piece of junk as a trade-in and not lose money. It also allows them to make a substantial profit when they resell cars that are in good condition. Unfortunately, not all car salesmen have integrity. Some take advantage of people by offering ridiculously low offers for trade-ins which allows them to earn huge profits.
- If a dealer offers a guaranteed trade-in price for any car, it means the price of the car on the lot is overinflated. For instance, if they offer $4,000 off the sticker price, regardless of the condition of your trade-in, you know that you have some room to negotiate even without a trade. However, if your car is in poor condition and you probably could not find a buyer, go ahead and trade it in. At least they take away your headache.
- If you do not have the time or patience to sell your older car through a private sale, then perhaps you might consider trading in your car, but be sure to get as much for it as you can. One advantage of trading in your car is that the money is applied to the purchase of your next car before sales taxes are calculated. So, if you trade in a car for $3,000 on a car valued at $13,000, you will only pay sales tax on $10,000.

7) ***Determine your insurance payment before you buy a car.*** You may be able to afford the car of your dreams, but you may not have enough in your budget to pay for the insurance. Sports cars and luxury models always cost more to insure. Additionally, a Toyota or Honda will be

NOTES

more expensive to insure than a typical Dodge or a Ford. Get the VIN of the vehicle you are interested in purchasing and call your insurance agent for a quote to prevent buying a car that you cannot afford to insure.

Review Questions

1. What is the key word in Proverbs 11:16, and how can we apply it to our spending? retain – keep your dignity and your cash
2. How can we change our thinking about shopping? rethink sales events, be patient, avoid paying full price, do your homework
3. Explain impulse buying? answers will vary
4. How can buying conservative clothing save money? it does not go out of style quickly
5. If you are trying to save money, why should you avoid buying a brand-new car? New cars depreciate in value more quickly than used cars.

Notes

Chapter Fifteen

Talk It Over

Key Verse: *"Where no counsel is, the people fall: but in the multitude of counsellors there is safety"* (Proverbs 11:14).

Introductory Thoughts:

- Earlier, we discussed the folly of impulse buying. Before making major financial decisions, always seek good advice. The verse listed above states that *people fall* when they have no counsel.
- Never let pride or self-sufficiency prevent you from seeking help with your money.

1. Talk to God

- Is God really concerned about our money? Having read most of this book, surely you have realized how much the Bible has to say about money. He is very interested in how you earn it, give it, spend it, and save it.
- Obviously, the most important One to consult with your finances is the Lord. We ought to pray about everything, including our money. Paul exhorts, "in every thing by prayer and supplication with thanksgiving let your requests be made known unto God" (Philippians 4:6). Prayer is the key that unlocks answers from heaven.
- Solomon wisely instructed, "In all thy ways acknowledge him, and he shall direct thy paths" (Proverbs 3:6). If you want to know how to handle your money, ask God. Every day many questions arise, "Should I buy this or that? Is it time to invest or wait? How much should I give as an offering?" How can we make the right decisions about our money? Here's the answer: "If any of you lack wisdom, let him ask of God, that giveth to all *men* liberally, and upbraideth not; and it shall be given him" (James 1:5).

Notes

- You might say, "I know all of the verses that you keep quoting about prayer." Great! Now apply them to your finances and rely on the Lord to help you make sound decisions. He promises to direct you and provide wisdom. One way that God gives us wisdom is through other people. If we seek good advice, compare it to Scripture, and pray about it, God will give us wisdom to make the right choices.
- If you need more than wisdom, God is able to help you with that, too. He promises to assist the less fortunate. "For he shall deliver the needy when he crieth; the poor also, and *him* that hath no helper" (Psalm 72:12). If you are poor or needy, be sure to talk to God about your situation!

2. Talk to Yourself

- Many foolish purchases can be avoided by simply asking yourself a few simple questions. Before spending money, run through this little list in your mind and answer each question honestly.

a. **Do I have the money set aside for it in my budget?**

b. **Do I absolutely need it, or merely want it?**

c. **If I buy it, will I have enough money for my other expenses?**

d. **Will it glorify God or my flesh?**

e. **Will it prevent me from giving to a need that God has impressed upon my heart?**

- Taking the time to ask these questions may prevent an unwise purchase and accumulation of unnecessary debt. It can also spare a lot of embarrassment as you avoid wrong decisions.

3. Talk to Your Spouse

- When a husband and wife work together, things are more apt to go smoothly. God created a pattern for each home that works wonderfully when followed. The husband is supposed to lead, and his wife is supposed to follow (Ephesians 5:22-28). Since the husband is also commanded to love his wife, he is responsible to lead her in the way that is best for her. Let's consider a couple of typical scenarios that reveal how important it is for both husband and wife to fulfill their respective roles.

Notes

- Our first example deals with a man who wants to buy a new gun. His wife wisely reminds him that the washing machine is on its last leg and will soon need to be replaced, suggesting that he should wait to buy his gun. Shrugging off her input might make him feel like "the man," but he would do well to remember that she might be right. While it is true that "the husband is the head of the wife" (Ephesians 5:23), every man should remember that his wife is a gift from God and is "an help meet for him" (Genesis 2:18). A good husband leads in the area of finances, but he also realizes that his wife was given to him by God to assist him. It may appeal to a man's ego to run roughshod over his wife, but doing so is not Scriptural. If every husband took the time to discuss financial decisions with his wife, not only would it prevent him from making some foolish decisions, it could also prevent hurt feelings and misunderstandings.
- The second example involves a wife who loves to shop. After establishing a family budget, her husband provides clear instructions about how much money she can spend in each category of the budget. Knowing that she only has $50 available for clothing, she decides to splurge a little and spend $100 because she found a good sale. She believes that, because she has been working hard at home, she deserves something special. At the grocery store, she overspends by $75 because she neglected to make a grocery list and ended up loading the cart with nonessentials. By the time she gets home, she has put $125 on the credit card with no means to pay it. Needless to say, her husband is upset because she did not follow his instructions. Her self-will and insubordination puts the family in debt and causes a rift in the marriage.
- Don't forget that one of the leading causes of divorce stems from money problems in the home. If both husband and wife follow God's model for marriage, they can prevent becoming another statistic. By learning to discuss your finances as a couple and work like a team, you can have a happier and more financially secure marriage. Instead of hiding things from one another, be transparent. Help each other fight the temptation to spend carelessly. If you invest more time encouraging your mate, you will have less time to blame him/her for all of the family's financial woes. There must be unity in the home. Further, by working together on the finances, you will both be better prepared for the time when

NOTES

one of you is no longer able to help. For instance, it becomes very difficult on widows and widowers if they were never involved in discussing money matters.

- Both the husband and wife must be familiar with the family budget, bank accounts, and investment portfolios.

4. Talk to Spiritual Leaders

- God gives us spiritual leaders to provide us with guidance. Since money has moral implications, do not neglect seeking advice from your pastor.
- The writer of Hebrews exhorts, "Obey them that have the rule over you, and submit yourselves: for they watch for your souls, as they that must give account, that they may do it with joy, and not with grief: for that *is* unprofitable for you" (Hebrews 13:17). Since God's men *watch for your souls,* you should submit to their Biblical counsel.
- Although you may be more inclined to follow the advice of a professional financial planner, a good pastor will provide a spiritual component to his counsel that secular men do not understand.
- Further, an experienced pastor has usually helped many others with similar problems that you currently face.
- Just remember that your spiritual leaders *watch for your souls as they that must give account.* Part of their job is to help you through difficult situations in life, including money problems. Besides, most of our money problems result from spiritual problems such as covetousness, lack of self-control, and failing to follow God's will.
- Truly, you need spiritual solutions to spiritual troubles. When you fail to submit to Biblical principles, *that is unprofitable for you.* So, don't be afraid to talk to your pastor about your finances.

5. Talk to the "Experts"

- Professional financial planners study current economic trends and investment opportunities for a living and can provide helpful strategies for you to consider. Obviously, finding the right one is extremely important. Thankfully, there are some good Christian professionals who guide people with godly principles and often share the values of their clients. If you find such an adviser, you may experience greater peace of mind than by working with a nonbeliever. However, that

NOTES

does not mean we should completely disregard financial observations made by non-Christians. Believe it or not, unbelievers often follow Biblical principles because those principles work. Therefore, you are not disobedient to Scripture when following advice from a financial consultant that is consistent with the Bible.

- It is true that we should never follow ungodly counsel, but that does not entirely prohibit us from seeking the advice of unsaved people. If that were the case, you would have to be sure that your mechanic was saved before you consulted with him about your vehicle. Additionally, you would be hard-pressed to get technical support over the phone for any of your electronic devices since many of the technicians are unbelievers. By allowing the principles of God's Word to guide you, you will be able to discern which professional advice is safe to follow.
- In the parable of the unjust steward, we gain some insight about worldly wisdom: "And the lord commended the unjust steward, because he had done wisely: for the children of this world are in their generation wiser than the children of light" (Luke 16:8). Unsaved people can be quite wise in financial matters; but when their motives and methods are unjust, their wisdom can be "earthly, sensual, devilish" (James 3:15). If a consultant's values are not consistent with the Bible, his priorities and advice will be skewed. Before seeking professional advice, be sure that you understand Biblical principles and determine to follow them first and foremost. When a secular man's advice falls in line with the Bible, you can prayerfully consider it.
- Unfortunately, some "experts" are driven by what is best for them, not what is best for you. Because securing your business provides financial planners with more income, the temptation exists to suggest options that are more lucrative for themselves than for you. Whether choosing a life insurance policy, developing an investment portfolio, or deciding between a will and a trust, you have many options. For instance, a whole life insurance policy may not be what you need, but a salesman may try to convince you to purchase it over a term policy because he will receive a higher commission. In a similar way, an estate planner may guide you to choose a trust over a will because he will make

NOTES

a significantly higher amount of money. Of course, this does not mean that every professional is out to cheat you.

- Be sure to do your research before seeking advice from a professional and develop a working knowledge of the topics for which you seek help. Walking in and saying something like, "I have no idea what I am doing. Can you help me?" is not a good idea. Those words leave you vulnerable to unscrupulous consultants.
- Finally, find a consultant who is more interested in teaching you about financial matters than he is about selling a product to you. You need to be educated, not merely persuaded. Someone who takes the time to educate you usually has your best interest in mind. To find a professional with a good reputation, ask people you know and trust.

6. Talk to Successful Friends

- Successful people are effective for a reason—they work at it. Any serious Christian who is trying to be a good steward is always on the lookout for ways to save money and manage their assets wisely. Chances are that many of your friends have learned valuable lessons about money from which you could benefit. A wealth of information is waiting to be discovered! Everything from how to get cheap airline tickets, stores that run the best sales, car dealers who are trustworthy, tips on saving energy at home, deals on meals, mechanics who charge a fare rate for labor, tips on running a budget, etc., are just a question away. Why not ask each of your friends, "What are the five best secrets you have found that help you save money?" Take their answers and make a list of ideas that will help you.

Review Questions

1. According to Proverbs 11:14, what provides safety? a multitude of counsellors
2. How can talking to yourself help you to avoid unwise purchases? answers will vary
3. Why should husbands and wives discuss finances? to work as a team and to avoid conflicts and divorce
4. Why can spiritual leaders provide financial advice? answers will vary – God gives them wisdom, they know the Scriptures, they have experience helping others

Notes

5. What are some things that are important to keep in mind when seeking counsel from professional financial advisers? be sure that they do not get you to violate Biblical principles, be careful that they are not motivated by what is best for them instead of what is best for you

CHAPTER SIXTEEN

MAKE AN EXIT PLAN

Key Verse: *"Thus saith the LORD, Set thine house in order; for thou shalt die, and not live"* (2 Kings 20:1).

NOTES

Introductory Thoughts:

- An exit plan is a comprehensive strategy to leave the ownership of a business. Key legal, financial, and tax questions are asked and answered to prepare for a smooth transition. If the corporate world sees the value of planning ahead to depart from a business venture, shouldn't every individual prepare to depart from this life?
- As someone once said, "There are two things that are certain in life—death and taxes." Concerning death, God has told us that "it is appointed unto men once to die, but after this the judgment" (Hebrews 9:27). Since we are going to die, we should make a financial exit plan to ensure a smooth transition of our wealth to those we leave behind.
- In the Bible, God included an example of one who needed to make an exit plan. Isaiah the prophet instructed King Hezekiah to prepare for his coming death. Not all of us get an advanced warning about when we are going to die, but we do know that the event will eventually happen. Accordingly, we would do well to consider the instructions given to Hezekiah—*Set thine house in order; for thou shalt die, and not live.* Because the purpose of this book is to discuss Biblical principles for money, we will limit our considerations about planning for death to financial matters.
- Here are the basics to remember as you prepare your exit plan.

1. PLAN TO HAVE ASSETS TO LEAVE

- I am not suggesting that you should have a goal of being rich before you die. However, I believe it is important to provide for your family to the best of your ability, especially in light of this sobering statement: "But if any provide not for his own, and specially for those of his own house, he hath denied the faith, and is worse than an infidel" (1 Timothy 5:8). By faithfully giving to God and managing the rest of your money, you should be able to leave something for your family when you die.

- Leaving an inheritance was important in Solomon's day. He said, "A good *man* leaveth an inheritance to his children's children" (Proverbs 13:22). An inheritance often included land and livestock, providing tangible assets that could be passed on from generation to generation. Though not everybody in our society has a family farm and our economy is more complex than in Solomon's day, we are not excused from planning to leave our family with an enduring inheritance. Allow me to suggest three ways we can accomplish this goal.

a. Home Ownership

- While it is not always possible for every family to own a home, it is a primary means of providing for your loved ones after you die. Purchasing a modest home allows you to retain part of your earnings as you build equity. Further, owning your own home can provide a sense of security to your family if you die unexpectedly. However, leaving an unmanageable mortgage payment with no means to pay it will do the exact opposite. If you choose to purchase a home, be sure that you also leave your wife with a source of income to pay off the house. That leads us to the matter of life insurance.

b. Life Insurance

- Securing a substantial life insurance policy can relieve your loved ones of tremendous pressure when you die. The amount of insurance that you will need varies with each individual, depending on the age and number of your children as well as your financial obligations. Experts recommend obtaining an insurance policy with a value of five to ten times your annual salary. A good policy will enable a wife to pay off the house and take care of the children if her husband dies prematurely. Couples with children should also consider a policy on

NOTES

the wife in order to leave the husband with sufficient resources for childcare in case of his wife's death.

- Unfortunately, 4 out of 10 adults in our country do not have life insurance, and only 1 of 3 couples with minor children has coverage.[33] Even many of the people who do have insurance have too little. Young couples may offer the excuse, "I can't afford it right now," but it is amazing how they can afford non-essential electronic devices. The fact is that we spend our money on what is important to us. If providing for your family's future in your absence is important, you will find the money for it.
- Two basic categories of life insurance policies exist: permanent and term. Permanent life insurance provides lifetime coverage as long as premiums are up to date, and term insurance only covers a set number of years. The two types of permanent insurance are whole life and universal life. The basic difference between whole life and universal life is that universal life offers more flexibility to the insured, allowing him to change the death benefit and alter the size and frequency of his premiums.
- In addition to lifelong insurance, a permanent life insurance policy offers another feature that term insurance does not—a savings/investment component. In other words, part of your premium goes toward the face value of your policy, which is the amount your beneficiary receives upon your death. The other portion of your premium is invested by the insurance company, and you earn interest which builds cash value. It is important to note that many experts believe that permanent insurance is a poor retirement investment because of the typically low interest that is offered. Another characteristic of permanent insurance is that you are allowed to borrow money against the cash value portion of your policy. Such a loan usually offers lower interest rates than banks and does not require a credit check. Some only recommend permanent insurance to a person who is younger and plans to keep the policy for his entire life.
- The most popular type of life insurance is term life. While permanent life insurance offers some attractive features, it is also very expensive. A term life policy is

NOTES

much cheaper because it provides only a death benefit with no investment component, meaning that the insured accumulates no cash value. However, many people believe they are better off investing their money in a good mutual fund rather than in permanent insurance because the potential for investment growth has been historically higher in mutual funds. Depending on your age, the best options for term life insurance are usually 20-year or 30-year terms. Premiums are dependent upon your age, current health, and lifestyle. For instance, if you are an overweight 55 year old who smokes and has high blood pressure, you will pay much more than a 30 year old who is a non-smoker in good health.

- What happens when your term expires? You have a couple of options. If you are in good health, you can purchase another term, either with your current insurance company or by shopping around for a new policy from a competitor. Because you will be older when purchasing a new term life policy, you will pay higher premiums. So, determine how long of a term you will need. If you have invested wisely and have your house paid off before you retire, you may not need much life insurance after you retire. If you are in poor health when your term policy expires, you may not qualify for a new term policy. In this case, consider converting your current term life policy to a permanent life policy. Many insurance companies allow you to convert your term life policy, but you have to do so before the term expires. If you choose to convert, remember that your premiums will dramatically increase; but this may be worth it if you still need life insurance.

c. Retirement Savings

- As mentioned in a previous chapter about investments, it is wise to invest part of your income in order to have sufficient funds when you retire. Since you are not guaranteed to survive to retirement age, it is helpful to list your beneficiary on each investment account. This will provide for a smoother and faster transfer of funds after you die. Unfortunately, if you have not carefully invested your money, you will have little or nothing to leave as inheritance for your loved ones.

NOTES

2. Make a Plan to Distribute Your Assets

- Now that we have considered how to ensure that you have something to leave for an inheritance, let's consider making a plan for what to do with that money. In the legal world, preparing financially for one's death is called estate planning. You do not have to be rich, own a home, or possess land to have an estate. Whether you realize it or not, you already have an estate and anything that you own is part of it. Even something as simple as a watch, ring, or piece of furniture qualifies as part of your estate. If you do not want your property and wealth to end up in the wrong hands, you must have a plan in place before you die. So, let's cover a couple of items that can help you with making plans for your estate.

a. A Will

- A will is a legal document that allows you to determine how your assets will be distributed upon your death. More importantly, a will enables you to appoint guardians for your children who are still minors. In addition, you can declare which individuals will inherit special family heirlooms. If you die without a will in place, the fate of your assets and children is determined by the courts. If you think that you can better decide such matters, make a will and put it in writing! As the testator, you assign an executor who will carry out your wishes expressed in the will. When choosing a guardian, discuss with your spouse who you believe best shares your values and love for your children. Be sure that the executor and guardian are willing and able to assume the responsibilities you are asking them to fulfill.
- To ensure a quicker transfer of some of your assets to your loved ones, name them as beneficiaries on your retirement accounts, pensions, and life insurance policies. This can avoid the time that it takes for the will to go through probate.
- Leaving no written directions for your hard-earned money is irresponsible, and making no provisions for the care of your wife and children is treasonous. Having a will is more than a good idea; it is a necessity. If you have known for a while that you should make a will, stop making excuses and do it. As you can see, having a will

NOTES

is of utmost importance. Believe it or not, almost 70 percent of Americans die without a will in place to direct where their assets will go.[34] How foolish! "Therefore to him that knoweth to do good, and doeth it not, to him *it* is sin" (James 4:17).

b. A Living Trust

- Another way to manage your assets is to develop a living trust. Two types of trusts exist: revocable and irrevocable. With a revocable living trust, you transfer your assets into the trust and remain in control of them as the trustee. Revocable trusts are more common. An irrevocable trust allows you to give away your assets permanently before you die, allowing you to exclude those assets from your estate. Some elderly people choose an irrevocable trust to avoid spending the majority of their assets on nursing home care before qualifying for Medicaid, which enables them to leave a larger inheritance for their beneficiaries. Such a plan could be a little tricky because Medicaid has a five-year look back policy which will check to see when you transferred your assets into the trust. If they were put into an irrevocable trust within five years' time, you may not qualify for Medicaid. Once a person transfers their money into an irrevocable trust, they have no access to that money. So, proceed with caution, especially if you think you may need the money in the future.
- A living trust differs from a will in a couple of ways. First, it allows you to manage your estate and benefit from it while you are still alive, whereas a will only goes into effect after you die. Second, your estate passes directly to your beneficiaries without going through the court system. Third, because you avoid probate, the record of your estate remains private. Not everybody wants their financial matters to become a public record. For people with a large amount of assets, a living trust is often recommended. Because setting up a living trust can be much more expensive than making a will, be sure that a trust meets your needs before rushing into one.
- In conclusion, a person may have a will and use one or more trusts to ensure that his assets are distributed properly. Do your research and consult a professional to

NOTES

determine what is best for you in your situation. It is not good enough to agree that you should make a written plan for your estate; you must be determined to work on it right away.

c. Power of Attorney

- If you ever become incapacitated and cannot make decisions for yourself, a power of attorney can make medical and financial decisions on your behalf. For instance, if you get dementia, you will eventually need someone to pay your bills and manage your finances. Theoretically, a power of attorney can spend all of your money on their own personal matters, leaving nothing to take care of you. Therefore, be sure that you appoint someone you trust implicitly.

d. Estate File

- When you die, you will not be around to show everybody where all of the important financial documents are located. In some cases, spouses may be completely unaware of insurance policies, bank accounts, and investment portfolios. It is wise to make a master list of every account and policy so that all of your financial information is easily accessible to your loved ones when you die. Put it in a folder and label it something like *Estate File*. It would be terrible if your family missed out on something such as a supplemental life insurance policy they never knew you had.

NOTES

Review Questions

1. What are some basic assets that are good to leave behind? a house, insurance policy, retirement savings
2. According to Hebrews 9:27, what is inevitable for everyone? death
3. What is a will? a legal document that describes how you want your assets distributed upon your death
4. Why is a will important? If you do not explain how you want your assets distributed, the court system will decide for you.
5. How can an estate file be helpful to those you leave behind? It provides information for all of your important financial documents.

---

[33] Jay MacDonald, "Survey: How many of us have life insurance? And how many have enough of it?" *Bankrate.com*, accessed July 9, 2015, http://www.bankrate.com/finance/insurance/money-pulse-0715.aspx.

[34] Dave Ramsey, "The Importance of Having a Will," *Dave Ramsey*, accessed July 6, 2015, http://www.daveramsey.com/blog/the-importance-of-having-a-will/.

CHAPTER SEVENTEEN

TEACH YOUR CHILDREN

Key Verse: *"Train up a child in the way he should go: and when he is old, he will not depart from it"* (Proverbs 22:6).

Introductory Thoughts:

- Children are like sponges and are able to absorb more information than many adults. Therefore, the best time to teach principles about money management to someone is while he is young. Those who are not taught key lessons about money at an early age are more likely to experience financial problems as adults. If you never learned how to handle money as a child, it is likely that your parents never had much training on the subject either. Thankfully, you can change your children's financial future by teaching them sound Biblical principles, which will enable them to escape some of the financial pitfalls that you may have encountered. Because you can affect the next generation, this might possibly be the most important chapter of the book.
- Illustration – Dave Olson relates, "My father instilled some very good principles into my life when I was a boy. He taught me to work hard, do a good job, and be persistent. When I was thirteen years old, I wanted a job at a local campground, which had a little restaurant, convenience store, and miniature golf course. The state law required that children could not enter the workforce until they were fourteen. My father told me, "The squeaky wheel gets the grease. If you want a job, you have to go down and let the owner know you are really interested." So, a month or so before turning fourteen, I went down and explained to the owner that I would soon be old enough to work. I returned once or twice more before my birthday to remind him that I was almost available for employment. Sure enough, I got the job, making a "whopping" $2.15 per hour. My dad's advice worked, and that principle has helped me ever since.

NOTES

Soon after I started working, it was my mother's turn to teach me an important lesson about finances. She took me to the bank and helped me set up a savings account. By the end of the summer, I was able to buy some new school clothes and had some money in savings. At an early age, I had learned how to get a job, work hard, and start saving. I am greatly indebted to my parents for instilling those traits into my life. My point is that lessons we learn as children will stick with us, just as the Bible says.

Unfortunately, bad habits also follow us into adulthood. Despite what I had learned about working and saving, I never learned how to establish and follow a budget. Instead of controlling my money, it began to control me. My $2.15 per hour wage seemed like big money, and I loved to spend it. As soon as I got paid, I would go to a place called The Game Room where I spent much of my income on video games and shooting pool. Because I did not have a budget in place, much of my earnings were squandered. Though my parents warned me not to blow all of my money, I had no mechanism in place to help me direct my finances. Throughout my teen years, I got used to spending most of my income on things that brought immediate pleasure; and my savings were hindered.

By the time I got married, I still had never made or kept a budget. Although I had learned to forego spending money on pleasure items, I had still had not learned to manage my money properly. As you can imagine, I began to live paycheck to paycheck and got into debt. When emergencies arose, I was not prepared. I recall one particular example. My wife and I were chaperones on a teen trip out west, and one of the activities included whitewater rafting on the Colorado River. After hitting one of the rapids, the boat my wife was in flipped over, throwing her into the raging waters. My boat was just behind hers, and I was able to be the hero and rescue her. However, when she came out of the water without her glasses, reality hit me right away—I didn't have any money to pay for new glasses. If we had budgeted our money, we would have had an envelope from which we could have pulled cash to meet the need. Instead, we went into debt, spending money that we did not have. After a few similar incidents, it did not take long to be in financial trouble.

Had I learned to set up a simple budget and plan how to use my money when younger, it would have been a habit already set

NOTES

NOTES

in place by the time I had reached adulthood, potentially sparing me a lot of grief. I am living proof that a child proceeds in the way he is trained. In the same way, you will either prepare your children for a bright future or enroll them in the school of hard knocks. Failing to train your children in the way they should go is basically synonymous with training them in the way they should not go. As a father, my goal has been to teach my children the right way to prevent them from having to learn the hard way. Don't you want to spare your children much trouble? If so, determine to get your financial situation under control and teach them simple lessons at an early age. Truly, they will not depart from it!"

- The following principles that we will discuss are not new. In fact, we have already covered most of them earlier in this book and have applied them to your life. Now, let's look at them in a new light—as they pertain to your children. Somehow, many adults fail to take what they know and teach it to their children on a level they can understand. I hope these ideas will be a help to you as you teach your children important lessons about money.

1. Work Hard

- Hard work is a fundamental principle required for money management.
- Illustration – Dave Olson explains, "Though I did not learn the specifics of budgeting as a child, I was taught something of greater value—a work ethic. Because I learned to work hard, I was able to adopt better money habits as I got older. This is probably the most important lesson I learned as a child. I praise God for a hardworking father who not only challenged me but also led by example."
- Consider the following verses about work, and notice how they relate to a person's financial standing. "Wealth *gotten* by vanity shall be diminished: but he that gathereth by labour shall increase" (Proverbs 13:11). In other words, those who work hard will tend to increase their wealth. "Love not sleep, lest thou come to poverty; open thine eyes, *and* thou shalt be satisfied with bread" (Proverbs 20:13). A person who won't get out of bed and go to work will end up poor, but those who learn to rise and put their hand to the plow will *be satisfied.* One of my favorite verses concerning work is Proverbs 13:4, "The soul of the sluggard desireth, and *hath*

nothing: but the soul of the diligent shall be made fat." Lazy people want things but cannot get them because of their laziness, but diligent people are filled with life's blessings. Here's a statement that sums up the correlation between work and financial success: "In all labour there is profit" (Proverbs 14:23).

- Teaching a child, therefore, to work provides an invaluable foundation upon which he can build. Even if you fail to teach him everything he needs to know in life, he will find a way to make it in the end. The words in the previous verses show the benefits of work: *increase, satisfied, fat,* and *profit.* Teaching a child to work is better than all of the economic lessons you can find in a textbook because without diligence, a person will not apply those lessons to daily living. How diligently have you taught your children to work? Be sure to make it a top priority!

2. Set Up a Budget

- Some reading this chapter are probably saying, "Come on Dave, my kid doesn't have much money." That is exactly why they need to set up a budget! Because they do not have much, they must learn to make it last; and only wise planning and spending can help them get the most out of their money.
- Just as you have to exercise restraint from spending all of your cash, your children must learn the same lesson. Saving is a sign of strength, and strength comes from exercise. Therefore, determine to teach your children to exercise restraint in their spending habits. The best way to do that is by following a budget.
- We have all heard of kids whose money "burns a hole" in their pockets. Unless I had something important to save for, I was one of them. As a young boy, I went down to Bill's Candy Store and loaded up on penny candy when I got a little money. Perhaps you were like me. The point is that kids shouldn't have a lot of money in their pocket unless it is there for a predetermined purchase. If you allow your children to continually spend money, they will take that habit into adulthood.
- Helping your children to develop a simple budget will give them good practice for their future. Using a modified version of the envelope system that we discussed earlier will provide a great visual aid for your children. Putting money into

Notes

envelopes allows them to see where their money is going. If they want to spend money on something and the envelope is empty, they learn quickly that they cannot make the purchase. Be careful not to yield to the temptation of giving them a "loan" because they will also learn that they can get things on credit. The "buy-now-and-pay-later" mentality is picked up at a young age, too.

- You do not need many envelopes to start with. Here are a few suggestions: offering (tithe and special offerings), gifts (e.g. Christmas and birthdays), savings, and spending. As a parent, help them determine what envelopes to create. Instead of doing it for them, sit down and ask them what things they need money for. You may have to suggest some things to be sure they don't miss anything important. For instance, in June, they are not thinking about buying Christmas presents; but teaching them to save a little bit each time they get money will allow them to buy their own gifts when Christmas rolls around. What happens when kids fail to budget anything for Christmas presents? Mom and dad give them money to buy gifts, thinking they are helping them. However, those kids do not enjoy giving presents to loved ones as much as children who use their own money.
- Likewise, those who learn to save for special purchases will appreciate them much more. Take, for an example, a boy who wants a new baseball glove. If he works hard and puts money away into an envelope, he will learn to patiently save for what he wants. Once he gets the glove, he will take better care of it because of the effort that went into getting it. On the contrary, a child who is given everything he wants without having to work and save for it will not truly appreciate his possessions and will be careless with them.
- Obviously, factors such as age and cash flow will vary from child to child, leading to different budget categories and amounts to spend; but the principle of budgeting will become a lifelong habit if started early enough. Also, parents ought to play an active role in helping children decide how much money to put into each envelope. If left to themselves, most kids would put the largest chunk of cash into the envelope marked "Spending." Careful guidance will help instill proper values and priorities at an early age. As you can see, setting up a budget teaches more lessons than just how to control cash. It teaches responsibility, patience, and priorities.

NOTES

Children will also be challenged to consider the future instead of living for the moment. A child who can learn self-control and self-denial at a young age will be better off in every area of his life. Can you imagine what our children miss if we fail to teach them how to control their money? Get excited about teaching your children to be good managers of what God has entrusted to them.

NOTES

3. Give to God

- Unfortunately, selfishness is easier to learn than generosity. I recall a story that a mother told about her little boy. She had given him some money to put into the offering plate when it passed by; but when the plate reached him, he did not want to part with the money. His mother urged him, "Put your money in." She was shocked at his reply, "If Jesus is so rich, why do we keep giving Him all of our money?" A child's sinful nature makes him prone to be selfish. So, the earlier a child learns to give the better. While some are more inherently stingy than others, it should be noted that many people learn to be tightfisted because they were never taught the joy of giving. Exercising the grace of giving will provide children with opportunities to prove Christ's words to be true, "It is more blessed to give than to receive" (Acts 20:35).
- In the beginning, your children should be taught three basic principles about giving: the tithe is the Lord's (Leviticus 27:30), giving brings more joy than receiving (Acts 20:35), and God provides for those who give to Him (Philippians 4:19). Obviously, as they grow, you will have opportunities to teach them many additional lessons about giving; but these are essential.
- Right from the beginning, you should teach your children to give one tenth of everything they get to the Lord. If Suzie gets a card in the mail from Grandma for her birthday with $10 in it, help her by exchanging the ten dollar bill for ten ones. Then, show her that one of those dollars belongs to God and ask her what she thinks she should do with it. If you have taught her properly, she will know she should give it to the Lord. After setting aside one dollar for God, you can explain that she should make a plan for the remaining nine dollars. Thus, the budgeting process starts immediately.
- In many ways, your children learn to give from you. When they watch you put money into the offering each week at

church, it shows them that giving is a priority in your life. They also see the sparkle in your eye when you give to a missionary project or special need in the church, which teaches them how joyful the experience of giving truly is. At family devotions, you can explain to them how giving helps missionaries tell others about Jesus or how the offerings help pay for the buses that pick up boys and girls for church. When teaching my children, I have often followed up with questions like, "Don't you think it is good that we give so others can hear about Jesus?" Remember, kids like questions. Not only do they like asking them, they learn a lot when you ask them to think about what you have just taught them. Lead your children to come to the conclusion that much good comes from giving. Surely, they will learn to rejoice in giving.

- As they get older, they will begin to see financial needs that arise in your family. While it is not wise to cause your children to worry about your money problems, it is important to share with them how God provides for you. After going through a financial crisis, you can explain how God miraculously provided for you. Then share with them how God promises in His Word to meet the needs of those who give to Him. In this way, they will see that the Bible is not a fairy tale and that God is real. Don't you want to teach your children to trust in the living God? If so, teach them the blessings tied to giving and living by faith.

4. Save

- How much do your children know about saving money? Is it something they like to do, or would they rather spend their money as fast as they get it? They need to learn three basic lessons about saving money: why they should save, how much they should save, and how they can save. Let's consider each idea separately.

a. Teach Your Children Why They Should Save

- Of course, there are many reasons to save; and in a previous chapter, we considered a few of them. Now, let's revisit those points and apply them to the instruction of our children. As parents, our goal should be to make Biblical principles easy for them to understand. So, let's consider a couple of ways we can point them in the right direction.

Notes

1) ***Saving is wise to do.***
   - Why not open the Bible and teach your children about the subject of money? This can be done during family devotions. Read this verse and ask your children what they think it means: "*There is* treasure to be desired and oil in the dwelling of the wise; but a foolish man spendeth it up" (Proverbs 21:20). They may struggle getting the first part of the verse. However, you can point out that wise people have treasure because they saved some of their money. The second half of the verse is easy—fools spend all their money. If your kids learn that, it will encourage them to not spend everything they get. Ask them, "Do you want to be wise or foolish?"
   - Just explaining a verse will not make children become savers. You must look for opportunities to apply truth to their lives. When they get some cash, ask them what they plan to do with it. They may say something like, "I am going to tithe and then get something at the store." Here's your opportunity! Ask them, "What kind of person spends all of their money?" Get them to think about what God's Word teaches. When they realize that fools tend to spend all of their money, they will look at you and say, "Oh, I guess I should save some." Teaching them the Bible in family devotions is great, but helping them to apply it to daily life is even better.
2) ***Saving empowers.***
   - Teach your children that if they learn to save, they will have money for things they want to do in the future. In Luke 14:28-29, Jesus taught the importance of planning in order to have enough money to finish a building project. After reading the account, you could ask your children what a person has to do to have enough money for what he wants to do. Obviously, he has to save enough money before he can have what he wants. Again, show your children that those who save can accomplish much in life. You can even share a few examples from your own life.
   - Illustration – Dave Olson remembers, "As a child, I loved riding my bike and sailing through the air off

NOTES

jumps. One day, while at Sears, I saw a five-speed bicycle named *Spyder 5*. Most kids in my neighborhood only had a single-speed bike, so the prospect of getting a fast bike really sparked my interest. My dad saw how the bike caught my eye and helped me devise a plan to get it. He saw it as an opportunity to mold my life. I was only about seven years old, but he taught me to work and save for it. I'll never forget—I went door to door taking orders for engraved metal social security cards. After that, I went through the neighborhood asking for odd jobs. When I didn't feel like working, my dad simply said, "If you want that bike, you are going to have to work for it and save your money." It seemed like a long time, but the time finally came to go back to Sears and buy my very own *Spyder 5*. Two words still ring clear to me today: *work* and *save*. I had learned that saving money allowed me to get something that others only dreamed of having."

- As your children learn to save, they will be empowered to make dreams become a realities. Giving them a taste of what saving money can do for them will inspire them to continue setting funds aside for important things in life. As they mature as Christians, their values will guide them to save for items that matter most. Saving for a bike as a child may seem vain; but if it helps him learn to save for a house as an adult, he will have learned an invaluable lesson. A person who saves will be empowered to provide for his family, give to the Lord, and help those in need. Aren't you excited about preparing your children to do that? If so, make saving a priority to them.

3) ***Saving prepares for the future.***
   - Because our nation was founded upon godly principles, we have been blessed with tremendous prosperity. However, we cannot expect God to continue to pour out His blessings on such a godless society. There is a direct correlation between moral and economic downfall. With recent attacks on the traditional family and intolerance of Christian views, I foresee hard times coming for our nation.

NOTES

Consequently, our children will undoubtedly face struggles that we have never experienced. It is our job as parents to teach our children to save so that they will be prepared for future difficulties. If we fail as parents, our children will be part of a growing number in our society that will not be prepared for a financial crisis. We must teach them to save for the future. I am not suggesting that you paint a picture of doom and gloom to your children, but you should point out to them that God will one day judge our nation for its wickedness. In simple terms, you can teach them that if they spend all of their money now, they will have nothing later when greater needs will arise.

4) ***Saving enables giving.***
   - Teach your children that their savings plan does not always have to involve a purchase for themselves. Hoarding money is selfishness and can be linked to greed and covetousness. Children should learn to put some of their money aside to give to God and to do things for others. For instance, they can save money to give for a special Christmas offering at church. Also, you can encourage your children to save up to get something nice for a loved one. Why not suggest to your kids to put some money aside to buy mom a pretty bouquet of flowers for Mother's Day? As they save for the flowers, they will be thrilled about surprising her with something special. Not only will they learn to give to others, they will also see the value of saving for things that are important.

b. Teach Your Children How They Can Save

1) ***The first introduction to savings for most children is the piggy bank.***
   - When they get money, they are taught to put it in the piggy bank until they need to buy something. Although that is fine for smaller children, older ones will need more direction than that. Allow me to suggest two simple ways to teach your children to save: set up a budget and establish a savings account.
   - Once again, I remind you of the importance of using envelopes to budget money. In a very real sense,

NOTES

budgeting is saving. After all, when your children put money into an envelope, they are reserving it for later use. For example, each time they place a little cash in the "Gift" envelope, they are actually saving for the time that they will need to buy Christmas or birthday presents.

- As I illustrated earlier, you can establish an envelope for a special purchase that your child is saving up to buy. Maybe your son wants a fishing pole. As he gets a little cash here and there, he should be taught not to neglect his other envelopes just because he really wants to buy the fishing pole. With patience, he will eventually have enough in the envelope and be able to make his purchase. A great sense of accomplishment will well up in his little heart as he walks out of the store with his very own pole bought with his own money. He will learn a lot more from that experience than the child whose parents buy him everything he wants.
- I honestly believe it is good for children to see that their savings pay off. It is also good for them to make some mistakes.
- Illustration – Dave Olson states, "I recall a lesson one of my teenage daughters had to learn the hard way. She had wanted a bicycle, and while out shopping one night as a family, she saw one that she liked. Because she did not have her money with her, she asked if we would pay for it and she would pay us back when we got home. I asked her if she had enough money for it, and she assured me that she had plenty. Once we got home, reality set in. Although she had the money, it was all that she had. She had a chunk of money that she had never distributed into her envelopes. So, once she paid us back, she had nothing for her other expenses, and she was unable to do some things she wanted to do. Her purchase brought regrets instead of happiness. Thankfully, that experience showed her that she needed to budget and save more wisely; and now she is quite thrifty. It is hard to watch your children make mistakes, but it is better that they learn before the stakes are higher."

NOTES

2) ***The second way to encourage your children to save is by establishing a savings account at a local bank.***
   - I am fully aware that savings accounts do not yield a high interest rate. However, the purpose for a child getting a savings account is primarily to teach them the habit of saving money. You do not have to make a special trip to the bank every time they have a dollar to deposit. Instead, a few times each year you can make a big deal about taking them to the bank and depositing money that they have put in the "Savings" envelope. It may be a lot easier to take the money to the bank and do it yourself, but the impression it makes on a small child is huge.
   - <u>Illustration</u> – Dave Olson recalls, "I still remember going into the bank with my very own savings passbook and thinking that I was doing something important."
   - As your kids get older, you can help them diversify their savings with other investment programs if you want; but a simple savings account can be helpful for starters. Do your children have a savings account? Do you ever take them to the bank so they can deposit their money?

c. Teach Your Children How Much They Should Save

- Children are able to save a larger percentage of their money than adults because they have fewer expenses. They don't have large recurring expenses such as housing, utilities, insurance, groceries, and transportation. Because children live simpler lives, they are able to save more. Therefore, instead of allowing them to spend "extra" money, teach them to save it.
- It may be hard to explain to a six year old that he needs money for college, but he can understand saving for a soccer ball. When kids are young, they need to have something more tangible to save for. Further, the concept of having money set aside for a "rainy day" is beyond most little ones. They might ask, "Why do I need money to spend if it is raining out?" So, when kids are small, set some short-term savings plans that will allow them to reach specific goals.

NOTES

- The older a child gets, the more expenses he will have. So, teach your child at an early age to put as much in savings as he can. In most cases, children should be able to save 50 percent of their income while using the other 50 percent toward their tithe and other budget categories. As your children mature, they will begin to see the wisdom in having money set aside for the future. The important thing is to get them started saving right away.

d. Saving Produces Other Benefits

- Saving involves choices. Each time a child decides to save for one thing, he decides to have less money for other things. By guiding your children in the decision-making process, you will help them to establish right priorities. When a child learns to prioritize properly, he has been given a skill that will help him throughout his entire life.
- Teaching your children to save money furnishes them with another great lesson—self-denial. Instead of saving money, this generation is obsessed with spending. That is because covetousness has a grip on spenders. By helping your children to form the habit of saving money, they will learn self-control and escape the bondage that covetousness brings.
- Isn't it amazing how applying one Biblical principle leads to other right actions? Certainly, every Christian parent should recognize the importance of teaching their children to save. I hope we will be more diligent in instructing our children to save money.

5. Avoid Covetousness

- Teach your children about the dangers of covetousness. When speaking to His disciples, Jesus said, "Take heed, and beware of covetousness" (Luke 12:15). If God warns His children about it, we ought to caution ours, too.
- You might think that covetousness is typically a problem found in adults, not children. Have you forgotten how your child started reaching for things on store shelves when he was only two years old and tried to fill the cart with what he wanted? Or, have you failed to remember that two words children learn early in life are *mine* and *more*? Mankind is

Notes

inherently selfish, and that characteristic leads to covetousness.

- Covetousness is not just an "adult thing." You must realize that your children will be tempted to covet. For this reason, you must never forget that covetousness is a sin; and consequently, your children need to be protected from its enslaving power. That means that you have to curb it in your own life. If your children see you craving more and more, they will follow your example. For instance, a mom who loves to shop at the mall will create a daughter who loves to do the same.
- As we discussed in an earlier chapter, the opposite of covetousness is contentment. Don't allow your children to be discontented with what they have. Those who give their children everything they want are promoting covetousness. Learn to say no to your child. They will be more appreciative of the things they have and be less apt to long for more.
- <u>Illustration</u> – Dave Olson relates, "Because my wife and I do not continually splurge on our children, they are more thankful when they receive something special. As a parent, I try to point out on a regular basis how good God has been to us. I honestly believe that when they are reminded of His blessings, it is much easier to be content. Try it with your children."

CONCLUDING THOUGHTS:

✓ Your children are counting on you. Not only must you learn how to manage your money, it is vital to teach your children how to do likewise.

✓ If you make a mess of your own finances, you are paving the way for your children to experience the same failures. However, passing on the lessons you have learned will prepare your children to have financial victories. In short, your actions will either help or hinder their future.

✓ You don't have to be perfect, but you must be persistent to teach your children what you have learned. Will you do your part?

NOTES

Review Questions

1. What does Proverbs 13:14 teach about a work ethic? Lazy people have little, and hard workers have plenty.
2. What simple categories should be included in a budget for children? offerings, gifts, savings, spending
3. What two ways can you teach your children to save? piggy bank, savings account
4. What are some other benefits of saving? teaches decision making, self-denial, self-control
5. According to Luke 12:15, what should children be taught to beware of? covetousness

Chapter Eighteen

Trust and Obey

Key Verse: *"If ye know these things, happy are ye if ye do them"* (John 13:17).

Notes

Introductory Thoughts:

- The song *Trust and Obey* reminds us that true happiness comes from having faith in God and doing as He says. The lyrics are familiar to most Christians, "Trust and obey, for there's no other way to be happy in Jesus, but to trust and obey."
- By applying those two simple commands to our lives, we will find real satisfaction, even in our finances.

1. Trust the Lord

- In 1861, a preacher named M. R. Watkinson wrote the following to the Secretary of the Treasury, "One fact touching our currency has hitherto been seriously overlooked. I mean the recognition of the Almighty God in some form on our coins."[35] Less than three years later, our nation printed "In God We Trust" for the first time on a form of currency. That motto should serve as a reminder to every believer that our dependence must be upon God, not money or the government. Unfortunately, many American rely on their cash and/or Uncle Sam to meet their needs. Instead of looking to IRAs or government handouts to take care of us, we need to wholly depend upon God. Let this be your testimony: "My help *cometh* from the LORD, which made heaven and earth" (Psalm 121:2).
- In the days of Christ, the average person was not nearly as affluent as we are today in our nation. If you recall, Jesus taught the people to pray, "Give us this day our daily bread" (Matthew 6:11). In many parts of the world, people live hand to mouth, struggling to satisfy their immediate needs because of a lack of money. They literally need to pray for

each day's provisions. To pray for *daily bread* should not be seen as a curse but as an opportunity to rely on the Lord. Even if you are blessed with much, you should still pray to God on a daily basis for your necessities. If you do not, you fail to demonstrate faith and dependence upon God. The apostle Paul had learned to trust the Lord regardless of how much he possessed. He testified, "I have learned, in whatsoever state I am, *therewith* to be content. I know both how to be abased, and I know how to abound: every where and in all things I am instructed both to be full and to be hungry, both to abound and to suffer need" (Philippians 4:11-12). When your satisfaction comes from God, you become less dependent upon material possessions. If you are happy when you have a lot of money and depressed when you have little, you have not learned to trust God.

- Following all of the principles found in the Bible does not exempt you from financial difficulty. While it is true that God teaches us to control our spending, give generously, save for the future, and stay out of debt, it does not mean that you will never have money problems.
- The Lord may test your faith with a financial trial. All we have to do is consider the account of Job. He was a godly man who had many material blessings. However, the Lord allowed him to lose everything. Notice his response, ". . . the LORD gave, and the LORD hath taken away; blessed be the name of the LORD" (Job 1:21). Like Paul, Job was able to praise God in times of plenty and in times of poverty. Although Job's wife told him to "curse God, and die" (Job 2:9), he resolved, "Though he slay me, yet will I trust in him" (Job 13:15). Because he leaned upon God, "the LORD blessed the latter end of Job more than his beginning" (Job 42:12). Never lose faith when a financial trial enters your life. God's purpose is to draw you closer to Himself; and as you depend upon Him more, you will see how He faithfully meets your needs. You can have peace and joy despite negative circumstances. Let "In God We Trust" become more than a motto—make it a way of life.
- You might say, "If I live by faith, then I don't need to worry about budgets, savings, or investments. Right?" Wrong! Living carelessly can hardly be considered faith. Since faith is based on obedience to the Word of God, it is very tangible. Those who claim to have faith must be obedient to His

NOTES

precepts. After all, "faith without works is dead" (James 2:26). If we truly trust in God, we will follow His commands regarding money.

NOTES

2. Obey without Delay

- Though many books have been written on the subject of money, the most reliable source of information is the Bible. When you study the writings of men, you get ideas; but when you study the Bible, you gain wisdom by which to live. The purpose of this book is to inform readers about the Biblical principles regarding finances and challenge them to follow. Along the way, I have provided suggestions on how to apply God's truths to daily life. However, you may find other effective methods to implement these principles. Just be sure to do what God says! Forgetting my anecdotes and examples is of little consequence, but forgetting the Biblical truths that have been presented will lead to money problems.
- Hopefully, you are more informed about what to do to get your finances in line with the Bible. However, knowing what to do is not enough; you must put it into practice. Jesus told His disciples, "If ye know these things, happy are ye if ye do them" (John 13:17). True happiness comes from obeying what God tells you to do. So, what has God prompted you to do in the area of your finances? Has He challenged you to set up a budget, get out of debt, tithe faithfully, save for the future, plan your estate, and/or teach your children about money? Instead of becoming overwhelmed by the amount of work ahead of you, take one step at a time. Before long, you will notice that you have travelled far down the path toward financial peace.
- I know a successful man who struggled financially even though he had a good job. One of the reasons that his finances were in trouble was because he had never set up a proper budget. After he began faithfully controlling his money, he was able to pay down his debt and enjoy life much more. Instead of being defeated by his money problems, he developed a plan and gained a great victory. Although he had known for years that he needed to set up a budget, he never got around to it. Now he regrets having put it off for so long. Dave Ramsey aptly said, "If you keep doing the same things, you will keep getting the same

results."[36] However, by implementing the principles of God's Word, you can completely transform your finances.

- Now that you know what to do, don't put it off any longer. "But whoso looketh into the perfect law of liberty, and continueth *therein*, he being not a forgetful hearer, but a doer of the work, this man shall be blessed in his deed" (James 1:25). Only a *doer* is blessed. David recognized the link between trusting and obeying. He said, "**Trust** in the LORD, and **do** good; *so* shalt thou dwell in the land, and verily thou shalt be fed" (Psalm 37:3, emphasis added). Did you notice the key words: *trust* and *do*? In order to be blessed in your finances, you must implement what you have learned. Your happiness depends upon your obedience.

"If ye know these things, happy are ye if ye do them"
—John 13:17.

NOTES

REVIEW QUESTIONS

1. According to John 13:17, what is the outcome of knowing and doing what God says? happiness
2. According to Psalm 121:2, where should our help come from and how can we apply that to our lives financially? the Lord – we should rely on Him for our provision, not government handouts or our investment portfolios
3. In Matthew 6:11, what did Jesus tell people to pray for to show daily dependence upon Him? bread
4. According to Job 13:15, what should our attitude be in the midst of trials (including financial ones)? trust God
5. David taught that we should, *"Trust in the LORD, and do good"* (Psalm 37:3)

.

[35] "History of 'In God We Trust,'" *U.S. Department of the Treasury*, accessed July 16, 2015, http://www.treasury.gov/about/education/Pages/in-god-we-trust.aspx.
[36] Ramsey, *The Total Money Makeover*, 15.

THE GREATEST TREASURE

Introductory Thoughts:

- Throughout this book, we considered many great truths about money; but we would be remiss if we failed to discuss the greatest treasure available to mankind—eternal life. All of the money in the world cannot purchase forgiveness of sin or reserve a home in heaven. If we spend most of our waking hours chasing after material possessions and neglect our soul, it would be a grave mistake. In Mark 8:36, Jesus posed a riveting question, "For what shall it profit a man, if he shall gain the whole world, and lose his own soul?" Think about it—what could be more valuable than your soul?
- Thankfully, the same God Who provided instructions for managing our finances also left clear teaching regarding eternal life. Let's consider how we can gain this heavenly treasure.

1. REALIZE THAT YOU OWE A DEBT.

- The Lord Jesus taught that our sin is similar to a debt that is owed. Even the Lord's Prayer emphasizes the need to seek forgiveness of sin—"And forgive us our debts, as we forgive our debtors" (Matthew 6:12). Did you notice the phrase *our debts*? That reminds us that we are all guilty of sin.
- In fact, the apostle Paul told us the same thing—"For all have sinned, and come short of the glory of God" (Romans 3:23). Whatever you do, please do not neglect this debt.

2. REALIZE THE CONSEQUENCES OF NOT PAYING YOUR DEBT.

- Like any other kind of debt, sin has to be paid. With Almighty God as the Judge, it is impossible to escape a day of reckoning by neglecting your sin.
- While failure to pay an earthly debt may involve fees and fines, the stakes are much higher with the debt of sin.

NOTES

- God said that "the wages of sin *is* death" (Romans 6:23). The death referred to in this passage is of an eternal nature and is further described in Revelation 20:14—"And death and hell were cast into the lake of fire. This is the second death."
- In earlier generations, people who could not pay their debts were thrown into debtor's prison until their debts were paid; but there will be no escape from the lake of fire once judgment is passed. The only hope of avoiding eternal punishment is to settle your debt before you die.

3. Realize that you cannot pay your debt.

- When we get serious about dealing with our earthly debts, we begin to work hard at paying them off. However, that is not possible with the debt of sin.
- Forgiveness cannot be earned, and the Scripture clearly states that no amount of good works can settle our sin debt. "For by grace are ye saved through faith; and that not of yourselves: *it is* the gift of God: **Not of works**" (Ephesians 2:8-9, emphasis added).
- Though salvation is a free gift offered to you, it first had to be paid for. When Jesus died on the cross, He bore the penalty of your sin—"the LORD hath laid on him the iniquity of us all" (Isaiah 53:6). He paid a debt that He did not owe because you owe a debt that you cannot pay.
- Jesus was punished for your sin and offers you His righteousness and a new life. "For he hath made him *to be* sin for us, who knew no sin; that we might be made the righteousness of God in him" (2 Corinthians 5:21).

4. Receive the payment made for your debt.

- Although Jesus has already paid for your sin, you must receive Him as your Savior in order to secure the forgiveness that He offers.
- Perhaps you realize that your debt of sin is so high that you cannot possibly pay for it. If so, repent of your sin and turn to Jesus, asking Him to cleanse you.
- He promises, "For whosoever shall call upon the name of the Lord shall be saved" (Romans 10:13). I urge you to stop

NOTES

trusting your good works to pay your debt of sin and depend upon Jesus for forgiveness.

- Why not bow your head right now and ask Him to forgive you and change your life? By receiving Jesus, you will gain the world's greatest treasure—"the gift of God *is* eternal life through Jesus Christ our Lord" (Romans 6:23).

NOTES

Selected Bibliography

Bowman, George, *How to Succeed with Your Money*. Chicago: Moody Press, 1982.

Burkett, Larry, *Debt-Free Living*. Chicago: Moody Publishers, 2010.

——, *Get a Grip on Your Money*. Gainesville: Christian Financial Concepts, 1996.

——, *Money Matters for Teens*. Chicago: Moody Press, 2000.

Economides, Steve and Annette Economides, *America's Cheapest Family Gets You Right on the Money*. New York: Three Rivers Press, 2007.

Freshman, Samuel K. and Heidi E. Clingen, *The Smartest Way to Save Money: Making the Most of Your Money*. Los Angeles: Straightline Publishers, 2013.

Hunt, Mary, *7 Money Rules for Life*. Grand Rapids: Revell, 2012.

Knight, Walter B., *Knight's Treasury of 2,000 Illustrations*. Grand Rapids: William B. Eerdmans Publishing Company, 1963.

Ramsey, Dave, *The Total Money Makeover*. Nashville: Nelson Books, 2003.

——, *Financial Peace Revisited.* New York: Penguin Putnam Inc., 2003.

Spurgeon, Charles H., *Faith's Checkbook*. Chicago: Moody Press, 1992.

Webster, Noah, *Noah Webster's 1828 Dictionary of American English.* Franklin: e-Sword by Rick Meyers, 2000-2014. Digital Library.

About the Author

Since entering the ministry over twenty years ago, Dave Olson has served the Lord in many capacities. After heading up a Christian school, teaching on the college level, and serving as a pastor, God called Dave into missions. He and his family faithfully served the Lord as missionaries to Zambia, Africa, for ten years until a series of ongoing health problems and life-threatening illnesses led to their return in 2012.

In early 2013, the Lord led Dave to focus on a writing ministry, and his books are now used at home and abroad. Dave's experience as an educator and preacher has uniquely equipped him to communicate God's truths to people from every walk of life. In addition to his writing ministry, Dave also preaches in missions conferences, revivals, and special meetings across the nation.

Visit www.Help4Upublications.com for more titles.

Other Titles Available on www.help4upublications.com

Nobody is exempt from heartaches and hardships. Even great heroes of the faith battled their emotions. Throughout the history of the world, people have battled grief, discouragement, fear, and anxiety. When handled correctly, trials can draw us closer to the Lord and build our faith. Learn how to see your trials as God sees them and react as He has instructed. When you do, you will see brighter days ahead! (188 pages)

Reading the Word of God is the best way to start your day, and *Daily Light* can make it easier! This book can be used for either personal or family devotions to provide practical insight for daily living. It embarks on a journey through the New Testament, including one thought from an assigned daily Scripture reading designed to share either a challenge or a promise for the day. (204 pages)

Get ready to take a journey through many of the Old Testament books. *Morning Light* starts in Genesis and includes the books of the Law, History, and Prophets. A practical thought from an assigned daily Scripture reading will challenge you each day. Whether you choose to use *Morning Light* for personal or family devotions, you will develop a better understanding of the Bible and find practical insight for daily living. (206 pages)

The perfect way to plan your daily devotions! This spiral-bound book contains many devotional helps: prayer list pages, Bible reading schedule, journal pages, topical verse reference, dictionary of archaic words, and more. Great for all ages! (152 pages)

Have you ever wondered what God has to say about finances? It's time to learn the proven principles of Scripture concerning money management. *Money by the Book* provides Biblical solutions for you and your money. Chapters on contentment, giving, saving, getting out of debt, setting up a budget, teaching your children about money, how to reduce spending, and much more! *Money by the Book* is used as a textbook in Bible colleges. (246 pages)

Made in United States
Orlando, FL
04 November 2026

90202242R00116